The Man
in the Leather Hat

And Other Stories

The Man
in the Leather Hat
And Other Stories

Paul B. Long

BAKER BOOK HOUSE
Grand Rapids, Michigan 49506

ISBN: 0-8010-5631-4

Printed in the United States of America

to
Merry
my wife
my love
my best friend
my courageous companion
throughout the years of our pilgrimages

Contents

Foreword, *Paul G. Hiebert*   vii

Introduction   ix

1. Tshiela Harieta   1
2. Kalonda of Kangate   9
3. War in Tshimbumbula   17
4. Tshiaba Challenge   25
5. The Prince and His Power   29
6. Mungede Had No Son   35
7. Different Can Be Dangerous   41
8. Prayer and Patience   51
9. The Lion and the Leopard   57
10. The Man in the Leather Hat   63
11. Maria of Paradise   69
12. Back of the Rim Rock at Little Albert's   77
13. Where the Girls Are Called Maria   83
14. Dona Edite of Porangatu   89
15. Benigno and the World of Spirits   97
16. Javaé   103
17. The Faceless Fathers of the Kuruaya   119

Foreword

Few books will grip the reader interested in missions as powerfully as will this one. Much is written in the field—surveys, broad histories, analytical treatises, and planning manuals—but these do not show us the day-to-day experiences in the life of a missionary. Paul Long has the rare gift of recording such experiences in vivid detail, and of seeing in them the hand of God. This is a series of fascinating stories, but it is more. Each marks a moment with eternal consequences. The people whose lives were transformed by Christ in these pages live on in the many whose lives they later touched. Those stories we will hear only in heaven.

Taken together these stories teach us much about the way God carries out his mission on earth. He begins with committed people. As we read we become aware that the storyteller has a passion for evangelism that drove him to use every opportunity to make Christ known to people. And Paul Long had a love for these people—not only the upright, respectable citizens of the land, but also those used and discarded by society—the drunkard, the prostitute, the failure, the half-clad waif. He saw in these individuals the makings of the kingdom of God, and through the transforming power of Christ they did not disappoint him. It is this passion that must drive the church and the missionary if we are to be faithful to the task God has given us.

We also see that God works in unexpected ways. There is a place in missions for making and carrying out plans. It was this that made it possible for the Longs to serve in Congo and Brazil, and to chart their ministry. In the end, however, it is God who changes people's lives, and he often catches us by surprise. We are disappointed when a large meeting is unexpectedly canceled and only one most unpromising person is in the audience, but God uses him to plant churches where the missionary could never go. We are angry when the call girls try to drive the preacher out of town, not knowing that God will use them to build the church.

We see that missionaries are vital to bringing the gospel to new lands, but we also see that much of the work is done by native evangelists and new converts. It is this partnership of outsiders and local workers laboring together as one body that is the bridge over which the gospel passes from one culture to another. The success of the work depends to a great extent upon the quality of the relationships in this community.

Finally, we catch a glimpse of the excitement of missionary service. There is weariness, disappointment, failure, loneliness, pain, danger, sorrow, and even death. But there is an indescribable thrill in being called to be a part of God's mission to a lost world. I am certain that many who read this book will not only learn more about missionary life, but also be challenged to become a part of that great calling themselves.

Paul G. Hiebert

Introduction

To those of us who have climbed our mountain in life and have started down the back side, it is rewarding to pause and look back at the people and experiences which have enriched the difficult days of our climb. It is refreshing to remember the faces that shine on us from the past. They give us courage to press on to God's future, for

> . . . we, who with unveiled faces all reflect the Lord's glory, are being transformed into his likeness with ever-increasing glory, which comes from the Lord, who is the Spirit (2 Cor. 3:18).

People who are still climbing their mountain in life need all the help and encouragement they can get from those who reflect God's glory. I hope the real people and the true experiences introduced in the short stories that follow will bring both refreshment and encouragement to all who read and reflect on the mysteries of God.

> For God, who said, "Let light shine out of darkness," made his light shine in our hearts to give us the light of the knowledge of the glory of God in the face of Christ (2 Cor. 4:6).

1

Tshiela Harieta

Lay up for yourselves treasures in heaven, where neither moth nor rust doth corrupt, and where thieves do not break through nor steal: For where your treasure is, there will your heart be also (Matt. 6:20, 21, KJV).

Our first day among the Baluba people of the Kasai in Congo back in 1954 had been a long and difficult one. We had driven over dusty, sandy roads since early morning to reach our new home at the Bibanga mission station, arriving at dusk with three road-weary, dirty, and hungry children. The warm welcome by Africans and missionaries was appreciated, as was the bath, the feast of wild guinea, and finally, bed.

The children were safely tucked in with mosquito-net protection, and my wife Merry was almost asleep when I started to turn down the kerosene lamp to finally put an end to the long day. Then the back door opened. Bare feet padded along the back hall. Into our dimly-lit bedroom moved a graceful old African woman who was to become a powerful influence on our lives.

"*Muoyo tatu Kalambai*," she said. (The words meant "Life to you, father Kalambai"; that was my name among the Baluba people.) "I have come to bring you this present." In her outstretched hands was a small chicken.

Just what I have always needed, I thought, and wondered how Merry would like this one in her bed. But Merry wasn't a farm girl and had not yet developed sufficient appreciation for my farmer's humor to receive such a surprise.

The smiling old lady bowed and said, "My name is Tshiela. Your wife is also Tshiela. She is named after me."

"We are honored, *Baba* [Baluba for Madam, more or less]," I replied, and I thought the deal was closed. Little did I realize the financial implications of having my wife named after this interesting African woman.

"Your wife is Tshiela. I am Tshiela. She is named after me. I am your other wife," she said with the funny little laugh we would come to know so well. Quickly she turned and gracefully moved out of the room, down the hall, and into the night, leaving the back door open as she left.

"Who is this woman who calls herself my other wife?" I asked a fellow missionary the following day.

"Oh, she is one of our colorful characters around here, and her story is amazing," my colleague replied. "When you accepted the chicken last night you became more or less responsible for her."

"I appreciate your telling me that now," I answered. "What is her story, and what should I do now?"

It seems Tshiela Harieta had been the third wife of an important tribesman across the river in Bakua Kalonji. When her old husband died no one wanted her because she had given him no children. She was faced with the option of becoming a village prostitute or a medicine woman who talks with spirits. But prior to her husband's death Tshiela had heard the gospel from a visiting missionary and had acknowledged *Yesu Kilisto* [Jesus Christ] as her new Chieftain, thus becoming a member of the New Tribe. Transferred to this New Tribe, along with all the beauty of her

2

tribal culture, were the Christian virtues as they were understood among her people at that time: Tshiela did not want to become either a prostitute or a shaman in the village of her husband.

To become a medicine woman, Tshiela would have had to pass through initiation rituals. For those rituals, the strongest medicine person in the area is called to the village. This powerful spiritual leader, usually a man among the Baluba, calls together all the practitioners of native medicine and magic in his area. The village then goes into a five-day drinking *festa*. On the third day, amid much dancing and drum beating, a grave is dug about ten feet from the village spirit house. At dusk, after drinking all day, the candidate is forced to lie down in the grave and a mat is placed over the hole. After a period of very active and noisy incantations, large stones are piled on the mat, the hole is closed, and dirt is piled on the grave of the "departed." After two more days of drinking and dancing, the chief shaman calls the village together around the spirit house and calls out the medicine women who have remained secluded inside since the sealing of the grave. One by one the women come out of the holy house, with faces painted white and wearing flowing white robes. Finally the candidate—now a new member of the shaman society—joins the group, having come from "death" to "life." During the days of her "death," she has been instructed in all the necessary wisdom of her new profession.

"How does the person get out of the grave and into the spirit house?" I asked Tshiela one day when she was telling about the customs of her people.

"During the time the others are waiting in the spirit house, they dig a tunnel to the grave. When the mat is placed over the open grave, the candidate crawls through the tunnel to the house."

"What if she doesn't make it?" I asked.

"Then she doesn't come back from the dead," Tshiela answered with her characteristic laugh.

"Why didn't you want to be a medicine woman, Tshiela?"

3

"In the New Tribe, I talk only with the Holy Spirit, and through him, I talk with Jesus and with *Tatu Nzambi* [Father God]. All other spirits who talk with men are evil and come from the devil."

"Who is the devil?" I asked.

"He is the chieftain of all the dead spirits who are not in the New Tribe," she answered.

"How did you escape doing what the village leaders wanted you to do, Tshiela? I thought you had no choice beyond the two options they gave you."

"I went into the forest to pray. Then I ran away. I came here to Bibanga to join the People of God who live here in God's village. The People of God are good. They let me live here and help the people of my new tribe," she said with a cheerful laugh.

Tshiela worked at the hospital where Merry served as nurse and teacher. Tshiela's duties concerned poor, sick people who were unable to bring their family with them to help during their illness. (Each patient had to have someone to cook food for them and to help in any other way necessary.) When food ran short or ran out completely for the patients under her care, Tshiela went into action beyond her regular duties. Our home was usually her first resort, since she considered herself my "other wife." After all, was not my wife named after her? And had I not accepted the white chicken she had given me?

About three months after our arrival at Bibanga, Tshiela came to our door. "*Muambi* [Preacher], there is a very sick woman in the hospital who needs meat to get stronger. Can you give her meat?"

Meat was hard to come by in those days. I hunted for about half the meat we ate, and hunting in the Congo heat was hard work. Beef was transported by truck from a town some fifty kilometers away and then brought to our station by porters walking all afternoon carrying the meat in a box on a pole between them. (Sometimes the meat men

4

got drunk along the way and the afternoon hike became a two-day disaster.) Their arrival was usually announced by the smell of overripe meat, and the flies assured us that their precious cargo was still in the box. (We were always interested in seeing what was inside—it was never quite the same as what we had ordered.) Merry would bathe the meat with vinegar to cut the unwanted savors and we would try to get it cold in our kerosene refrigerator—when that appliance was working. Beef, well-cooked to disguise problems of overripeness, was a much-anticipated pleasure enjoyed only twice a week and we were not eager to share it with anyone beyond our family.[1] So Tshiela's request for meat to help a poor, sick woman I had never met nor cared to meet presented problems. "Tshiela, I have no meat for your friend," I said, being less than entirely honest. "I am sorry I cannot help you," I added, this time quite honestly.

"That is all right, *Muambi*," she answered. "I understand." Then, after some hesitation, she said, "I saw the white rooster I gave you in the pen when I passed. He is big now and ready to be eaten, isn't he?" Her happy, congenial laugh somewhat softened my anger. I was looking forward to that fat rooster for our Sunday dinner, and it was not easy to see him go to feed someone I had never met.

"Thank you, *Muambi*," she said, and she went happily on her way to the hospital to feed her sick patient in need of meat. I felt that Tshiela was making me a better Christian than I really wanted to be.

As the years passed Tshiela became thinner and thinner. She moved more slowly among her suffering patients. Merry virtually exhausted her vitamin supply trying to build Tshiela back to normal strength. Finally we discovered that she had been giving her food to the poor

---

1. In time, I would be able to build up a herd of cattle sufficient to supply some milk and meat for those villagers in greatest need, but that was not the case when we arrived. I would also be able to increase our chicken and rabbit production, but this too would take time.

patients, starving herself in the process. It took a lot of convincing to help her see that she could not continue helping others if she was not able to work. And helping others was her duty as a member of the New Tribe.

One morning Tshiela arrived in our yard with an old, naked woman. "Why did you bring this naked woman into our yard?" I asked with some irritation.

"She has no blanket, *Muambi*, and the nights are cold."

I was wiser now in the ways of African women and deeper in the customs of the Baluba people. Leaning on logic understandable to the Congolese, I answered, "Tshiela, this woman is not a member of the New Tribe. (Most of our Christians wore clothes by that time.) There are countless naked women all around us who have no blanket tonight. You would not want me to show *kansungasunga* [partiality], would you?" I knew I had her there, because partiality is looked upon unfavorably among the tribesmen.

"That is right, *Muambi*," she cheerfully replied. "You can't show partiality, and there are so many people who have need."

As she made her way down the path to the hospital, she was singing her strange, happy little song, and I had the feeling that I hadn't heard the last of the subject. As darkness settled over the Lubilash Valley and we were eating our evening meal, someone clapped at the door.[2] I went through the customary Congolese protocol until our caller identified herself as Tshiela.

Sensing problems, I said to Merry, "It's Tshiela. You had better take it. It's hospital business."

"No," said my usually cooperative wife, "this is your deal."

Outside on the back porch I found Tshiela squatting—

2. The Congolese always clap their hands to let you know they are there. The next step in the ritual is to ask, "Who is there?" The answer must be, "*Meme, munto,*" meaning "me, a person" (that is to make sure you are not being called by a spirit). "Person who?" is the next question. And the reply is the name of the person calling.

naked like the old woman who had come this morning. "*Muoyo* [life to you], Tshiela," I said in greeting, and she returned "life" to me.

"It has been a hot day, has it not, *Baba Tshiela?*"

"Yes, *Muambi*, it has been very hot."

"It looks as if it will get quite cool tonight, don't you think?"

"Yes, *Muambi*, it is already getting cold."

"Is that right? Then why are you naked, if you are cold?"

"I gave my dress away to the poor woman who was here this morning."

"Then I guess you will sleep cold tonight, Tshiela," I said with fine, manly firmness.

"Oh no, *Muambi*," Tshiela replied. "I gave my dress away because you could not show partiality to the pagan woman with all the others around us in need, and that is right. But I am of the New Tribe of the Jesus People and you could not leave me in need, could you?"

A little while later Tshiela padded down the path toward the hospital wearing a new dress and a new blanket draped around her shoulders. She thanked me with a happy laugh and departed singing her funny little song about the goodness of God.

"Thank you, God," I prayed, "for Tshiela, who helps us all to be better Christians than we would be without her."

Tshiela Harieta comes as near as any person I have ever met to following our Lord's command:

> "Lay up for yourselves treasure in heaven . . . for where your treasure is, there will your heart be also" (Matt. 6:20–21).

2

Kalonda of Kangate

Finally, be strong in the Lord and in his mighty
power. Put on the full armor of God so that you can take
your stand against the devil's schemes. For our struggle is not against flesh and blood, but against the rulers,
against the authorities, against the powers of this dark
world and against the spiritual forces of evil in the
heavenly realms. Therefore put on the full armor of God,
so that when the day of evil comes, you may be able to
stand your ground, and after you have done everything,
to stand (Eph. 6:10-13).

The African sun burned down upon us as we
climbed the mountain path to the village among the trees.
The people of Kangate, in the wild Babindi section of central Congo, seldom saw white men in those days, and excited cries greeted us as we entered the dusty streets
leading to the chief's harem. We had pushed over a hundred miles through bush country to answer a strange request from an old chieftain among these isolated people.

Several days previously a runner had appeared at our
mission station. "Teller of the Word," he had said, "Chief
Kalonda wants to talk with you."

What does the old rascal want to see us about? I wondered, and the question remained in my mind as we drove along dangerous roads through mountainous country toward his village, stopping several times along the way to rebuild log bridges spanning creeks too deep for our truck to ford. Now, with the village in sight, we would soon know the answer. Sometimes these urgent calls from isolated villages merely meant someone important wanted a ride to the mission station. What could Kalonda want with us?

In the shade of the chieftain's grass-roofed residence, and surrounded by the smaller houses of his several wives, sat an aged, emaciated man wrapped in an old blanket. Enthroned on a cross-legged stool bedecked with leopard skins, the sick and broken old chieftain lifted a feeble hand and greeted us with the customary salutations of the land: "*Muoyo wenu*—life to you."

"*Muoyo webe*," we replied. "Life to you."

Looking across the council ring at this once-powerful chieftain, I recalled the tales I had heard of what he once had been. Twenty years ago Kalonda was feared and respected for a hundred miles or more around his realm. As a bold, savage ruler he freely exercised the power of life and death over his subjects, and of death or slavery over his captives. His renown as a chieftain was surpassed only by his great power as a medicine man; leaders would come from distant villages to buy his charms and curses.

One day the chief of a neighboring realm, Kasenda of the Balubai people, arrived in the village of Kangate. He was worried and needed help.

"I have killed the money messenger of the mission and taken the money he was carrying to their preachers and teachers," he recounted. "Now the dead man has come to life and returned to the white men to tell what I have done. Give me medicine to make me invisible when the soldiers come!"

"Return to your country," replied Kalonda. "Get twelve she-goats; six young, strong women; ten spears and ten knives; then come back to buy my medicine. That is the price for medicine powerful enough to make you invisible."

Complaining of the high cost of the needed protection, Chief Kasenda returned to Balubai to round up goats, women, and weapons. Meanwhile Chief Kalonda proceeded to compound his promised medicine. Sending out his bodyguard, he directed the capture of a young woman from a neighboring tribe. In a short time the captive was brought before the chief. With elaborate ritual the chief's warriors cut off the captive's head, which was needed for Kalonda's "invisible charm." Cannibal ritual was also involved in the proceedings. On the appointed day, the medicine was presented, the goats and women and weapons were exchanged, and the deal was closed to the satisfaction of both leaders.

When the soldiers arrived several weeks later to capture the ruler of the Balubai, Kasenda quietly entered his house, picked up the head that he believed would make him invisible, and stepped out into his courtyard to laugh at the baffled troops who would not be able to see him. To his surprise, anger, and consequent regret, they surrounded him and bound him securely, then marched him off to jail. Still holding his high-priced medicine, Kasenda became enraged with his former friend whose charm had failed. He cursed Kalonda and gave his name as the murderer of the woman whose head he held in his hands. Kalonda, too, was captured and arrested.

At first condemned to die, both men were saved when their executions were three times postponed. Finally the sentences were changed to fifteen years in prison at hard labor. To these chieftains, this judgment was as harsh as death.

Released from prison because of failing health, Kalonda had come home to die; now, he wanted to talk with me. After the customary silence of respect, I began the conversation: "*Nfumu* [Chieftain], your runner says you want to talk with us. We have come. What do you want to tell us?"

Kalonda's reply startled us. "Tell me about the white man's God," he said.

11

"The God we follow is not a white man's God," I answered. "He is the Father of the New Tribe, his people. Jesus Christ is the great Chieftain of the New Tribe, and he accepts anyone who will follow him. My friends here are also members of the New Tribe. They will tell you about this New Tribe and how to become a member of it."

Our Congolese colleagues could readily understand the battle old Kalonda was now facing. Especially able to identify was Pastor Mutombo, a former African medicine man who had turned to Christ and now was able to deal insightfully with people trying to escape spirit control. He took over the conversation and I listened, deeply concerned over the battle taking place between the powers that are real and the liberation that is possible.

"You still trust in your medicine," said the pastor, observing the copper charm bracelets adorning the once-strong spear arm of the old chief. "Why do you ask about another god?"

With great reluctance, the old man slipped the bracelets from his arm, dropped them in the dust, and said, "Now tell me, 'Teller of the Word,' about your powerful God."

With those copper bands lying at our feet, I began to realize something of the price Kalonda was having to pay for what he asked. He had just renounced his potency, and I heard him mutter, "I used to have eight good, strong wives, and all but three old ones ran away while I was in jail. All I have left are old women who are too weak to work or have babies." My eyes followed his glance toward three old women crouched close to a nearby hut. They were agitatedly mumbling to each other, evidently unhappy with the events taking place.

"Your medicine couldn't hold your women while you were gone?" the pastor questioned; the answer was a grunt.

"Now," Mutombo continued, "the war medicine on your belt shows where you look for power."

After a long, thoughtful pause, the old warrior cut the small skin bag from his belt and dropped it in the dust.

"Now the 'counter-hex' packet at your neck?"

The old man put a trembling hand to the thong around

12

his neck. This little charm held his protection against all his enemies and made their magic of no power. Silently we waited until, at length, he broke the thong and let his "security" fall at our feet. Grunts of respect for his courage echoed around the ring of watching tribesmen.

"Your *Buanga bua Bunfumu* [medicine of chieftainship]," the pastor reminded.

Wearily Kalonda arose, entered his house, and returned with a large antelope horn filled with assurance of his power over his people. (I have never been sure just what makes up such powers, but have been told the horns hold bits of hair, the eye of a frog, the tooth of a lion, and the claw of a bird.) Lightning medicine followed, and a host of other protective charms which give forest people some respite from their constant fear of living.

"This is all the protection I have," Kalonda said. But Pastor Mutombo was evidently waiting for another, more costly surrender. "Now get your 'life charm,'" he said, "and I will tell you about the God of the New Tribe."

The old man trembled, broke out in perspiration, shook his head, and wrapped his tattered blanket across his bony chest. The three old wives had remonstrated with his renunciation of his medicines and, with this last demand, they commenced the death wail and started tossing dust in the air over their heads. At this acknowledgment of his impending death, Kalonda roused from his fearful reflections, reentered his house, and returned with a little packet of skins. With all the dignity of a great leader, he silenced the wailing wives and surveyed his council ring.

"Teller of the Word," he said, holding out his little packet in his boney hands, "you have asked for the life of Kalonda! This medicine has protected my life from all my enemies for many years. Many still live who hate me and have curses on my life. When I throw down this medicine all their curses will fall on me. My protecting spirits will withdraw their protection, and I will die. But Kalonda is not afraid to die!"

As the packet dropped in the dust, the old chieftain

13

straightened to his full height, lifted his old eyes to the distant hills, and waited for death. We sat in silence as the seconds grew into minutes and tension mounted in the ring of onlookers who waited for their chief to die.

After a long while, the old chief looked at us, and his lips parted in a relieved grin: "I'm still alive! Kalonda has not been struck dead!"

It took a long time to answer questions from old Kalonda and his people—questions, Kalonda said, about the God he had always feared but had never known. As the afternoon shadows lengthened, the old chieftain rose with dignity before his people. In a quiet, confident voice he announced, "Kalonda has a new Chieftain. I follow *Yesu Kilisto* and he will help me across the river, lead me through the dark forest, and take me to his village where I can sit with his people. I belong to the New Tribe. Kalonda wants all his people to follow *Nfumu Yesu* [Chieftain Jesus] and go with him to the Village of God."

When we left Kalonda we drove on into the country of the Balubai to see Chieftain Kasenda, who had shared the years in prison with Kalonda. One of Kasenda's wives was a strong Christian and several of his children had studied with us in mission schools. One of his sons was preparing for the ministry and we wondered what the return of the father would do to those plans.

When we reached Kasenda's village we were greeted warmly by members of the New Tribe, including the chief's Christian wife and children. We asked to see the chieftain.

"Kasenda doesn't want to talk with you," we were told.

"We have come to *ela muoyo* [give him life]," we said. "Why doesn't he want to see us?"

"Kasenda is a tired old man," said the Christian wife. "He rejects life and wants to die. He murdered the mission messenger and is ashamed to see you. He refuses to become a follower of Jesus Christ and only wants to die."

With sadness for Kasenda and gladness for Kalonda, we drove back home to mission headquarters at Bibanga. Not many days after our visit to the Babinde and the Balubai, a messenger arrived with the brief report: "Kalonda has gone on his journey to meet his new Chief."

The passage from bondage in the Old Tribe to freedom in the New Tribe is impossible without supernatural help. The powers we confront are beyond our abilities to overcome. Without help we are without hope. God reaches out to helpless people in Jesus Christ, enabling them to turn from the old ways of death to new ways of life through the power of his Holy Spirit.

Kalonda and Kasenda each had to make his own choice as to whom he would serve in this life and in the "unknown land beyond the river." *Yesu Kilisto* knows only two tribes: those who follow him, and those who reject him as their Chieftain.

> Put on the full armor of God, so that when the day of evil comes, you may be able to stand your ground, and after you have done everything, to stand (Eph. 6:13).

3

War in Tshimbumbula

I am sending you out like sheep among wolves. Therefore be as shrewd as snakes and as innocent as doves. . . . When they arrest you, do not worry about what to say or how to say it. At that time you will be given what to say, for it will not be you speaking, but the Spirit of your Father speaking through you (Matt. 10:16, 19-20).

Do not walk alone into Tshimbumbula, *Muambi* [Preacher]. If you do, you will never come out alive."

My secretary Ilunga was very much upset. He had listened to the message of the runner from the Christians of Tshitola: "Come to us, *Muambi*. There is war and we need your help."

"What can I do to stop a war between your people?" I asked the runner. I had no desire to become involved in fighting among the violent Africans of Tshitola, and the story of the runner left little room for hope.

"*Nfumu Mpingiabo* [paramount chieftain for the area] has accused us of not paying taxes to him. He captured six of our tribesmen and has murdered five of them. He

17

beat the last prisoner and sent him back to Tshimbumbula with his message for our Chieftain Mutombo: 'Pay the rent or die!'

"If you do not come, *Muambi*, there will be war."

"And if I come?"

"Perhaps there will be no war. Mpingiabo is your friend."

It was quite true that Mpingiabo was my friend. "But Mutombo of Tshimbumbula has never been very friendly with me or with the mission," I said. "What do you think I can do?"

"At least you can try," the runner said, and he left me.

Needless to say, I was not enthusiastic about getting involved in any war in Tshitola nor a visit with the chief in Tshimbumbula. I had enough war in World War II to last me my lifetime. Why get involved in this mess with so little chance of success? But the last words of the runner haunted me: "At least you can try."

True, I had worked with Mpingiabo for several years, helping him get started raising cattle to replace the vanishing wild game in his area, and helping train some of his people to take care of the growing herd. I had preached in his village and eaten in his large, grass-roofed residence. He had eaten in my home and discussed Christianity at great length. (The mission had an excellent evangelist and teacher working in his village, and several of his sixty wives were strong Christians.) I had spoken in his favor with the Belgian authorities and commended his administration. But I knew so little about his private life and the hidden methods by which he maintained control over the tribes under his authority. Perhaps, at least, I should try.

But when I invited my secretary to go with me to Tshitola, he assured me he was much too far behind in the work I had given him to be able to spare the time. I talked with the local pastor and several Christian leaders about going with me, but all shook their heads and said it was too dangerous and beyond their area of effective influence.

18

And they all repeated the warning of Ilunga: "Don't walk alone into Tshimbumbula. If you do you will never come out alive."

Accepting their warning, I drove to the home of a missionary colleague, Day Carper; shared the problem; and asked his advice. He had served much longer among the Baluba people than I had, was much deeper in the culture, and had known the two warring chieftains for years.

"There will never be peace between Mpingiabo and Mutombo," Day said, "but perhaps a real war can be averted. I'll go with you and we will try."

Our first stop on the way to the village of Tshimbumbula was with Chieftain Mpingiabo. We listened to his side of the grievance with the people of Tshimbumbula and their local chieftain, Mutombo. No mention was made of the murdered men of Tshitola.

Mpingiabo provided six men to go with us into the hills of Tshitola to Tshimbumbula. They were to help carry our equipment, show us the way, and help us cross the river into the area. None of these men were happy with the assignment. Elephants had left broken branches along our road, and several times we had to pull large limbs aside before our truck could pass. At the end of our road, the porters led the way along a narrow path through grasslands down to a swiftly flowing river much too deep to cross without a boat. We called for the boatman, but there was no reply. Finally, one of our guides found him hidden along the riverbank and brought him to us.

"Life to you, *Tatu* [Uncle—a term of respect in that land]," we greeted the old man. "Will you put us across the river?"

"No. I will not cross the river."

"We will pay you well, *Tatu*."

"No money will pay me to cross into Mutombo's land."

"Will you lend us your canoe? We will bring it back."

"If you cross the river, you will not come back," the old man said, and walked away.

One of our guides then left us, returning a while later

19

with an old dugout canoe. We crossed the river into enemy territory and started the long, steep climb to the village of Tshimbumbula. Despite the heat of the day and the difficult terrain, our guides walked very rapidly and we were unable to keep them in sight. Suddenly, rounding a bend in the mountain path, we found our equipment piled on the trail; the guides had disappeared. Well, I thought as we continued the climb alone, at least we won't have to worry about returning the canoe to the other side. The guides will do that for us.

Smoke was rising from several houses when we reached the village, but no one was in sight. African villages are usually alive, full of movement and sounds of life. But Tshimbumbula was as silent as a tomb when we entered. And I remembered the saying of old-timers in the land who warned, "When a village is silent, it is dangerous."

Day and I kept walking and talking, laughing a little to show anyone watching that we weren't afraid. After all, were we not responding to an invitation from Christians to come here?

In the center of the village we found a very large gathering of warriors. Seated on a stool which was covered with a leopard skin was Chieftain Mutombo. Neither he nor his warriors seemed very glad to see us, even though we knew they had been watching us since we crossed the river.

"*Muoyo Nfumu,*" we greeted. Life to you, Chieftain.

"Why have you come?" Mutombo roared. (It was very impolite not to "throw us life" in return for our greeting.)

"We have come to discuss with you the 'affair of God,' " Day replied.

"I have no time for the 'affair of God,' " Mutombo replied. "I am at war with Mpingiabo, and I will kill him and all of his friends. You are friends of Mpingiabo, and you will die."

We stood with our backs to a large medicine tree which stood in the center of the council ring. Warriors began to stamp their feet, shake their spears, and work themselves into an ugly mob.

20

Mutombo stood before us and shouted, "You are friends of Mpingiabo. Friends of Mpingiabo must die. I am Mutombo, Chieftain of the People of Tshitola. I have spoken. You must die."

I silently prayed, "Lord, please take care of Merry and the children, and of Day's wife and family also. And yes, please look after us now also!"

A promise from God suddenly came to my mind: "When they arrest you, do not worry about what to say or how to say it. At that time you will be given what to say, for it will not be you speaking, but the Spirit of your Father speaking through you." That promise was fulfilled for my colleague and me in Tshimbumbula; we both understood clearly what we should say at that moment and how to say it.

Day had to shout to be heard by all. "You are the Chieftain of Tshitola. You are the leader of this great people? I don't believe it." Then he turned to me, saying, "*Kalambai* [my name among the Baluba], do you believe the great people of Tshitola would follow a leader who does not follow the traditions of his people?"

"No. It cannot be," I answered.

Mutombo, half drunk on palm wine and dazed by hemp, stood before us puzzled. "What do you mean? What customs of our people am I going against?"

"We are guests in your village," Day replied. "We have come at the request of Christians among your people. We honor and serve the Creator God who made the people of Tshitola and who has made you their chieftain. But you cannot be their chieftain. You have turned your back on strong traditions of your people. You have failed to measure up to your chieftainship. You have failed."

"How have I failed?"

Day answered with a firm, strong voice. "We came to Tshimbumbula as friends, and you treat us as enemies. You accuse us without hearing our words of wisdom. You show us no hospitality. You offer us no food, nor the honor due a guest in Tshimbumbula. Can it be that the great people of Tshitola follow a chieftain who ignores the customs of his tribe? I just cannot believe it."

A miracle then took place in Tshimbumbula as Day Carper and I stood with our backs to the medicine tree, surrounded by angry, half-drunken warriors who were ready to kill on the chieftain's command.

Sacred customs rule the hearts of tribal people, and true leaders must be faithful models for those they lead. "I have done wrong," Mutombo said, shame and humility in his voice. "You are my guests. We will hear your words of wisdom. You will eat with us. And, when you are ready, you will go in peace. I, Mutombo, Chieftain of Tshitola, have spoken. It will be so." And Mutombo kept his promises as a true leader of his people must do.

God also kept a promise that day. He continued to make very clear to both Day and me what words we should speak to these angry people and how they should be spoken. And later that night the entire village gathered to hear the words of *Nzambi*, the Creator God, who had placed the people of Tshitola in their sacred lands. His words of wisdom counseled against war with Mpingiabo. Members of the New Tribe, the Christians in the village, counseled the people to pray and please God, and trust him to work out their serious problems with the paramount chieftain. The Belgian colonial government was appealed to. The case was settled, and there was no war, nor further bloodshed.

Along the uncertain trails of life each of us must enter our Tshimbumbulas. With great reluctance to become involved in battles we can avoid, we are deeply aware of our limitations to alter conflicts that seem to have no answers. "At least you can try," the runner had said to me. And, until we have tried, we never know what we can do. This lesson has stayed with me and has led me into many interesting experiences of trying to help. Some of these experiences were failures and others were victories that only the Lord could have brought about. But the greatest lesson that remains with me since my visit to

22

Tshimbumbula is the warning from wise African Christians: "Do not walk alone into Tshimbumbula. If you do, you will never come out alive."

By the promise of God, we did just that.

When they arrest you, do not worry about what to say or how to say it. At that time you will be given what to say, for it will not be you speaking, but the Spirit of your Father speaking through you (Matt. 10:19-20).

4

Tshiaba Challenge

The people walking in darkness have seen a great light; on those living in the land of the shadow of death a light has dawned (Isa. 9:2).

In the days of open range in Africa's Congo, halfway through the twentieth century, cattle owners trusted their herds to drovers who followed the feeding stock, kept them out of village crops, and returned them to the security of the home corral each evening. The mission station owned a herd of some 130 head of cattle which provided meat and milk for local needs and helped supply starter herds for tribes interested in learning how to take care of them. Our young stock was separated from the herd for about two years for weaning and growth, and the village of Tshiaba provided room for our calves to graze while Tshiaba men took care of the stock. It was my responsibility to check on them every three months or so, and I always dreaded the job.

To get to Tshiaba from our mission station at Bibanga required setting out by horse before four in the morning, crossing a swamp—populated with numerous hungry crocodiles—by sunup, and riding through the village to the corral before the cowmen left with the herd for the open range. Hungry cattle do not like to break their feeding schedule; if the herd was already in the high grass before I arrived, at least three hours were added to the day's work. Today I had arrived too late.

When we got the cattle back into the corral, I had to rope them from the ground, throw uncooperative two-year-olds, and then tie them down for necessary doctoring. Since it was beneath the dignity of our cattlemen to get their hands dirty with animals, I had to do the heavy work on my own.

Exhausted, I arrived back in Tshiaba before the women had returned from their morning's work in the fields. I joined the men in the shade of the council ring to sleep until the women had time to fix the big meal of the day. But when they arrived they saw my horse and demanded "a good word from God" while the food was cooking. I had not come to Tshiaba to preach and I needed rest for the long ride home. But my horse was resting, and she was the one with the most work left to do.

Most of the village gathered around expectantly to hear from God through his Word and his rather reluctant representative. I talked about light shining in dark places. I talked about life in the shadow of death. And I told them about Jesus who had said, "I am the light of the world. Whoever follows me will never walk in darkness, but will have the light of life (John 8:12).

Tshiaba was a dark place in the 1950s. Life was hard and survival was about all one could hope for. And people needed the other members of the tribe to survive. They had no medical clinic, no school, no teacher or preacher, and no Christian leaders. (One or two women who had been treated in the mission hospital were professing Christians.) Medicine women, under the direction of a strong regional medicine man, provided about all the security they had. In addition to native cures and traditional treatments, the medicine women claimed constant contact with the spirits of departed relatives and, upon occasion, immediate com-

26

munication with powerful supernatural spirits. Native practitioners were feared, respected, and for the most part disliked—but they were used when necessary.

An old woman, clad only in a breechcloth and squatting on the fringe of the listening circle, was one of the medicine women. Her angry scowl indicated her disapproval of everything I had to say. Evidently we were communicating with different spirit powers, and she resented the intrusion upon her turf.

"You lie, Preacher," she snarled. "You do not tell the truth. Stop your lies and go away."

I answered with more patience than I really felt. "Why do you say I lie, *Grannie* [a term of respect]?"

The old woman rose to her feet, stood tall with all the dignity of a gifted African orator, and said, "You say the people who have lost contact with the Creator God sit in darkness. And I agree. You say that *Nzambi* [God] still loves the lost tribesmen. That I do not know. You say that *Nzambi* sent his Son, *Yesu Kilisto*, from the Village of Nzambi to the lost tribes to call them back under his authority. And men killed *Yesu* and refused to come back to *Nzambi's* authority. That also I do not know. *Yesu* never came to Tshiaba. We did not kill him. You say that *Tatu Nzambi* [Father God] still loves his rebelling tribesmen and will forgive the murder of his Son. You say that *Nzambi* wants all of us to accept *Yesu Kilisto* as our new Chieftain and to become members of the New Tribe. Any one who is sorry for the bad things done in life can become the People of Nzambi. He will look after us in life. He will have someone on the other side of the River [death] to take us through the Unknown Forest and lead us to the Village of Nzambi where we can sit down with his people forever. This I cannot believe! It is too good to be true. You lie, *Muambi* [Preacher]. If all this were true, the People of Nzambi would have been here a long time ago to tell us about this Good News. You have come too late."

Gently I replied to the tall, old woman who had beautifully summarized my message. "But I have come today, Grannie. It is not too late."

"You came today to doctor your cattle. You stopped here to rest and to eat. You preached because you were asked to tell us good news. And you tell us lies. Go away. I do not believe you."

"The message is true, Grannie. Only the messenger is unworthy. It is not too late."

The old woman looked across the Lubilash Valley toward the distant hills where the mission station had served for forty years. Preachers, teachers, and evangelists had flowed from the center into more than twenty thousand square miles, reaching out to the scattered villages of many tribes and peoples. At Bibanga large schools offered the opportunity for young people to learn and develop skills. Advanced medical service was provided at the mission hospital, and rural clinics were set up in various locations. Yet Tshiaba had indeed been neglected in the busy ministry of the mission. Its people still sat in darkness.

"For many years now," the old woman continued, "we have watched the smoke rise from the village of the People of Nzambi up there on the hill. If the Good News you bring were true, the People of God would have been here a long time ago to tell us about it."

I have since traveled a long way from Tshiaba in the Lubilash Valley of the Congo in Africa. But I can still see a tall, old African woman wistfully watching the smoke rise from the village of the People of God. For her, the Good News was too good to be true. If it were true, we would have been there long before to tell her about it. For her, we had come too late.

Jesus, concerned for the people who sit in darkness, said

Let your light shine before men, that they may see your good deeds and praise your Father in heaven (Matt. 5:16).

28

5

The Prince and His Power

I saw Satan fall like lightning from heaven. I have
given you authority to trample on snakes and scorpions,
and to overcome all the power of the enemy; nothing will
harm you. However, do not rejoice that the spirits sub-
mit to you, but rejoice that your names are written in
heaven (Luke 10:18-20).

My first reaction to Mutombo's urgent message
was one of anger. "What's wrong with him?" I asked my
secretary. "Is he afraid of a stupid medicine man?"

Only two weeks earlier, Mutombo had moved to a small
village among the Baluba people of Congo in answer to
that community's request for a worker from our mission
to come and teach the *bualu bua Nzambi* (affair of God).
They had quickly met our requirements, constructing one
grass-roofed chapel for God and one house for the teacher.

When I moved Mutombo and his family into the new
work, the whole village took part in the celebration. Someone mentioned that the shaman was not happy with the
new turn of events in his village, but I gave little atten-

₋ion to his displeasure. (At that time, in 1955, I viewed native medicine men and women as simple power brokers working only in the realm of superstition; I was aware of no supernatural dimension to their "bag of tricks.")

Sitting with Mutombo in the moonlit yard after an evening service, I had been surprised to hear him say, "This problem with the shaman could be serious, *Muambi* [Preacher]. The power of the devil is very stong here."

Now, after only two weeks in the new village, Mutombo wanted to move out, and I couldn't imagine why he was afraid.

"Perhaps he knows more of the danger than we do," offered my secretary. "You'd better go with the truck to see what needs to be done."

I was still in my first term in Congo at that time and was not as deep in the culture as was necessary for the responsibilities placed upon me. My senior missionary colleagues were not in the field, and the older, Congolese Christian leaders were not within easy reach. Nor did I feel any necessity for their wisdom: Mutombo was simply afraid and all I had to do was encourage him to trust the Lord. It would be great for the village people to see the victory of his faith.

At least that is what I thought back then.

When I arrived with the truck at Mutombo's village, I found his belongings packed and ready to go. (That was unusual for the time and culture; often they had to harvest crops while I waited.)

"What is wrong, Mutombo? Why do you think you should run away from here?"

"The shaman has a curse on me."

"You can't just walk away because the shaman has put his curse on you. Think of what your fear of him will say to the people you are trying to reach for Christ."

"It's easy to trust when you don't know the danger, *Muambi*," my friend replied.

30

"Do you think you should run away?"

"If I want to live, I must go."

Turning to his wife I asked, "Do you think you should go?"

"Yes, we must go."

The *Capita* (head man of the village) came up about that time, and I asked, "Can you not control your shaman?"

His answer was clear: "No."

"Can you protect your teacher?"

"No. Only God can do that."

"Do you want him to stay?"

"Yes."

"If I stay, I die," Mutombo said quietly.

"Mutombo, I believe that the devil does not have power to kill a Christian. He can tempt and oppress, but not enslave or destroy a Christian. The devil's representatives are held back by the power of Christ in the lives of his followers. If you run away now, you will destroy the Christian witness in the village. The people will continue to fear the evil spirits and will see no hope for freedom in Christ."

"If you tell me to stay, *Muambi*, I will stay," Mutombo replied. "But my head and my heart tell me to move out with my family today."

There was much I didn't know at the time I encouraged Mutombo to remain in his village and face the shaman and his powers. For instance, I had no idea that native medicine men and women guaranteed their cures or curses. Patients paid in advance and dealers in native medicine could not afford very many failures. I have since been told that about 85 percent of African shamanism is based on native psychology which can cure or kill when properly applied. If the psychology death curse fails, poison is used, or properly executed accidental murder. But this explanation still leaves 15 percent of shaman power beyond natural, human explanation. More than half of the strong Congolese Christian leaders in our church had come to Christ from shamanism, and several had been noted medicine men. They all told me of communications they had experienced

31

with supernatural powers during the course of their pre-Christian practices.

Unfortunately, I knew none of this when I spoke to Mutombo that day when he was determined to leave the village. As I drove back to the security of the mission station, happy with the results of my visit, I thought about how his decision to stand his ground would convince many people of his village that Christ was greater than all the devils that surrounded them.

Less than twenty-four hours later, Mutombo was dead. Though it was the dry season at the time, with no rain or conditions conducive to electrical storms, he had been struck by lightning as he walked to the chapel to conduct morning prayers. A runner arrived at the mission with the message, requesting that I come and get Mutombo's widow and children.

When I got to the village, Mutombo had already been buried—where he fell, halfway between his home and the chapel—and his family was packed and ready to leave. No one seemed surprised about the incident but me. The Christian work in the village was over, never to be attempted again during our days in Congo.

I returned to the mission with Mutombo's widow and children, and I assumed financial responsibility for their care as long as I was in the country. When we left, they returned to their people. I do not know what has happened to them since.

The experience with Mutombo has taught me several lessons of great value:

First, never be heroic with someone else's life.

Second, knowledge is never a substitute for wisdom; when wisdom is lacking, seek wise counsel soon and follow it faithfully.

Third, cultural blind spots sometimes make it impossible for us to really understand another culture. I had been trained in the scientific system of western education in which all supernatural power is presumed to rest in God and anything that cannot be explained scientifically or accredited to God must be attributed to simple superstition. Just because I had not yet encountered the occult did not give me just cause for rejecting its possibility and potential power. Congolese colleagues knew the dangers better than I, and I should have consulted them.

Fourth, the experience with Mutombo has left me with a question: How much power does the devil have over the life of a Christian? The "prince of this world," as Jesus called the devil, is still active and very powerful. As a "roaring lion" (1 Peter 5:8), he is dangerous both day and night—always restless, always active, always ready to take advantage of his prey. He can tempt, but can he enslave? I know many Christians who are enslaved by vices they cannot escape without Christ's liberating power. The devil can enslave, but can he destroy? I know Christians utterly destroyed by the devil's vices. Does this mean that Christ does not have sufficient power to overcome the prince of this world?

Theologically, the answer is easy: "Do not be afraid, little flock, for your Father has been pleased to give you the kingdom" (Luke 12:32). Jesus said, "In this world you will have trouble. But take heart! I have overcome the world" (John 16:33). To his witnessing servants, Jesus said, "I saw Satan fall like lightning from heaven" (Luke 10:18). But the battle is still going on. Christians suffer. Christians are sometimes defeated. Christians die—some tortured, some murdered, some martyred. The victory is secure in Jesus Christ but the battle will continue until the King returns.

How much power does the devil have over the life of a Christian? Only as much as is permitted him by our sovereign God, in order to accomplish the hidden purposes of a loving heavenly Father. Satan has fallen "like lightning from heaven," but he is still the very powerful "prince of this world" who can be successfully opposed only through the power of Christ in one's life.

Mutombo, I should have listened to you, and my mistake cost you your life. But I have learned well the lessons you taught me and will be guided by your wisdom until we meet in God's Village together with all whose names are "written in heaven" (Luke 10:20).

6

Mungede Had No Son

The LORD spoke to me with his strong hand upon me, warning me not to follow the way of this people.... When men tell you to consult mediums and spiritists, who whisper and mutter, should not a people inquire of their God? Why consult the dead on behalf of the living? To the law and to the testimony! If they do not speak according to this word, they have no light of dawn. Distressed and hungry, they will roam through the land; when they are famished, they will become enraged and, looking upward, will curse their king and their God. Then they will look toward the earth and see only distress and darkness and fearful gloom, and they will be thrust into utter darkness (Isa. 8:11, 19-22).

Mungede had no son.

He had a happy Christian wife and two daughters, but no son.

He was director of the Boys' Home where some two hundred boys lived while they studied at the mission station, but he had no son.

He was the best hunter of wild guinea fowl in the

35

Bibanga mission area and he was an elder in the local church, admired and trusted as a Christian leader. But Mungede was not happy, for he had no son.

Although he was one of my first and best friends among Africa's Baluba people, and although we worked, talked, hunted, and prayed together, I did not realize how deeply Mungede was burdened and how heavy were the pressures from pagan relatives over his failure to father male offspring. Nor did I know, at that time, why a son was so necessary in tribal thinking. Therefore I was quite shocked when the pastor announced during morning prayers one day that Mungede had returned to his village and gone back to the old ways.

I just could not believe it. I thought I knew my friend. I thought we communicated on deep levels and shared openly with each other. But it was true—the tribal pressure for a son had forced him to leave his Christian wife who had given him only daughters, and to return to his village, taking on two younger women with the hope that they would bear him sons.

"Why are sons so necessary?" I asked the pastor.

"Daughters marry and go with their husbands to the village of his parents. Children all belong to the father—not the wife—in our customs. Only sons remain in the village, and only sons therefore can feed the ancestral spirits. If one does not show respect for his *Ba Nkambua* [dead ancestors], they will become angry and afflict the careless and ungrateful son. Furthermore, when a tribesman dies, he must leave a son to care for his spirit which remains in the village as an unseen member of the tribe."

"Then Mungede is trusting tribal ways more than the teachings of the New Tribe, isn't he?"

"Yes," the pastor replied, "he has rejected the commandment of God which warns against communicating with spirits of the dead. He has gone back to the old tribe and is now caught in its darkness."

I was determined to try and bring my friend back, so I traveled to his village, some five kilometers east of

36

Bibanga station. When I found Mungede, I was shocked with the change in his appearance. His once radiant face was dark with the "utter darkness" that marks the people under direct demonic direction. It was obvious that he had been talking with spirits and seeking their power in his life. But I had a problem. I did not believe that evil spirits could take over a life that had been transformed by faith in Christ. From a theological standpoint, it seemed impossible for the born-again believer to go back to his former slavery, but it looked like that was just what had taken place with Mungede.

We hunted guinea all day, rested in the shade, and talked at length about life, death, and our hope for eternity. But Mungede was as closed as any pagan I had ever talked with; I could not reach him in any way.

After a good hunt, we returned to his house to rest while his wives prepared the guinea hens for our evening meal. Looking around the area, I was impressed with the fact that he had settled in the very center of spirit worship for the tribe. A medicine man sat nearby, along with three medicine women in the robes worn when communicating with spirits. The drums were there, as were the rattles, the charms, and the spirit mound. The mound looked like a good pulpit to me, so I asked Mungede to beat the drum and call the people to hear a word from God.

"You want to worship here?" he said. "This is the devil's territory."

"I can talk with God anyplace, Mungede, and any time I please. Don't you know that?"

"We will see," he said as he pounded the talking drum. (I never learned to "talk" with the drum except to say, "Kill the rooster, the preacher is here." I left Congo before I was able to add, "but leave the setting hen on her nest.")

A large crowd gathered around the spirit mound. I was surprised to see that the medicine man and women were amused—it's always nice to have people happy when you tell them God's Good News, especially when they are capable of being dangerous.

When I stood to speak, I felt the oppressive presence and

power of overwhelming evil. The "utter darkness" was suffocating me. I felt the cold fingers of death press around my throat and I could not speak. As I stood there in foolish helplessness, the medicine people laughed; it sounded like voices from hell.

I turned in utter defeat to sit down with Mungede. "I can't speak here," I said when my voice returned.

"You should have known better. This is the devil's turf. You have no right or power here."

"Does God have any turf in this village?" I asked.

"Yes. On the other side of the village we used to have a Christian chapel. The building is gone, but the land still belongs to God."

"If you will invite the people to go with us there, I will try again." And when I passed the medicine man, I added, "Come with us, powerful one, and hear about the 'affair of God.'"

"I will stay on my turf," he answered. "Here I have power."

On the other side of the large village, I was led to a clearing where the outline of the former chapel was marked by a shallow ditch formed by rain washing over the grass roof. The rectangular outline was about ten feet wide and thirty feet long. I stood where I supposed a pulpit had been, invited the people to gather around, and noted with surprise that all those who had come with us—about seventy— were pushing to stand within the boundaries of the ditch. Apparently they wanted to hear God's word while standing on God's turf.

In the seven years we had lived with the Baluba, I had never preached with such liberty in God's Spirit. The words flowed with power, clarity, and beauty well beyond my normal abilities in that language. The people who stood on God's turf were electrified with a strange power and their response was immediate and unanimous. "We will rebuild God's house," they announced, and by evening of the next day a new grass-roofed chapel stood on the site of the former building. A new house for a teacher was also constructed, and God's work was reborn in the village.

38

Mungede never returned to the New Tribe during my days in Congo, but continued to follow the ways of his people, looking for a son to feed his spirit after death. Instead of inquiring of God, he consulted with "mediums and spiritists who whisper and mutter"—and demonstrate power enough on their own turf to shut my mouth. He consulted "the dead on behalf of the living" instead of going to the Word of God. He looked to those who "have no light of dawn," the ones who "will be thrust into utter darkness."

Two things I learned well in that village called Nkumba: never to invade the devil's turf without clear orders from the Lord, and to move out of enemy territory when the battle is beyond me. It does not pay to underestimate the opposition.

7

Different Can Be Dangerous

For you have spent enough time in the past doing
what pagans choose to do—living in debauchery, lust,
drunkenness, orgies, carousing and detestable idolatry.
They think it strange that you do not plunge with them
into the same flood of dissipation, and they heap abuse
on you. But they will have to give account to him who
is ready to judge the living and the dead (1 Peter 4:3-5).

Everyone in the village was dead drunk.
Every man, woman, and child was lying in vomit, completely unconscious, sleeping off the results of a three-day
drinking ritual. Even the dogs did not care enough to bark
at us, and some of the chickens staggered as though they
too had been in the mash.

The year was 1957. Pastor Katumpa and I had traveled
for several days over difficult roads and were deep in the
country of the Balubai; we were hoping to spend the night
here. During previous days we had left our truck when the
road ended, we had crossed a swift river in a borrowed
dugout canoe, and we had walked on a damp jungle trail
for several hours to visit this village where one of our mission evangelists was living and working.

"Where do you think our evangelist is?" I asked Pastor Katumpa with some concern.

"Would you stay in this village at a time like this? His wife would have been forced to take part in the sex orgies and he could well have been killed if he objected."

Katumpa then added words of wisdom that have stayed with me through the years: "It is hard and often dangerous to live a Christian life among violent, non-Christian people who rule their societies," he said.

It is indeed hard and often dangerous—and lonely as well. As we left the village to move on to an evening service and a night of rest elsewhere, a Tse-tse fly landed on my arm. Fortunately I was able to move him on before he bit me. (Some of the flies carried the dreaded sleeping sickness that was taking so many lives in that area during those days.)

"*Kalambai!*" Katumpa cried out, using my name among the Baluba. "Why did you send that fly back to me? He bit me."

"It was not his time to bite me, Katumpa. Be sure to see your doctor."

I forgot the incident at once, remembering it only when I heard the following year during furlough in the United States that Pastor Katumpa had died of sleeping sickness.

B ack in the truck we were hailed along the road by two women who had been waiting for our passing. "Pastor, stop to pray with Grannie [a term of respect]. She is about to cross the River and wants you to pray for her crossing."

It had been a long, discouraging day and I really did not want to pray with anyone. I wanted only food and sleep. So I said to the waiting women, "I don't know any Grannie here. Are there Christians in this village?"

"Yes, Grannie is a Christian. She is the only one in this village."

As darkness fell, Pastor Katumpa and I wearily climbed the steep bank to the lonely village and walked into an unforgettable encounter. In a small hut an old African woman lay dying. Her cold feet were pressed to the warmth of a smoldering wood fire that filled the room with smoke. She held up a feeble hand to greet us and, with a weak voice, said, "Thank you for coming, Pastors. I am going to cross the River and I want you to pray for me."

"What would you like us to pray for, Grannie?" I asked.

"Just tell my Chieftain Jesus that I am about to cross the River into the Dark Forest. I would appreciate him having someone there to meet me, and to lead me to the Village of God where I can sit down with all God's people in his presence."

"Where have you learned of the 'affair of God,' Grannie?" I asked. "I didn't know there were Christians here."

"Years ago a missionary came through here and told us the good news of the 'affair of God,' and I told *Nzambi* [God] that I would follow *Yesu Kilisto* [Jesus Christ] as my new Chieftain if he would accept me into his New Tribe. I have never known much about the customs of his tribe, but I have tried to please him and trust him even though it has been hard. Now I am going to see him and to find out if he will let me stay in his village."

Katumpa and I prayed for a dying woman who had stood alone in a pagan village and had tried to live by the light she had. People in her village said she had always been different since she joined the New Tribe several years ago. They said the reason she was different was that she had a new light and could talk with God. She did not have to go through the ancestors anymore to get to the Creator God.

"Good-by Pastors," she said as we were leaving. "Thank you for coming. I will now cross the River unafraid."

(When we arrived back at the mission the following week we were greeted with a simple message from Grannie's village: "Grannie has crossed the River and gone to the Village of God." It is difficult to live a godly life when one is surrounded by non-Christians whose lifestyles set the pace and standards for the village. "Grannie" had dared to be different. And she crossed her last river unafraid.)

W ho are those little people, and why are they looking so unfriendly at me?" I asked Katumpa as we sat discussing the "affair of God" with Christians in yet another village. The people in question had gathered at the edge of the village.

"They are the Batua [Pygmies]," Katumpa informed me. "And they don't like you."

"Why don't they like me?"

"Because you are white."

"What is wrong with being white?"

"Belgian state men are white, and the Pygmies don't like them."

"Why don't they like the Belgian state men?"

"Because they come to collect taxes, and Pygmies pay taxes to no man."

"Let's go over and talk with them," I suggested. "We can tell them I am not Belgian nor do I collect taxes. Then maybe they will become friendly and we can talk with them about God."

"If you go to them without invitation, they will kill you," Katumpa said. "They choose their own friends."

"Fine," I said. "Then you go to tell them we are nice people who wish them no harm."

"I will only go if they invite me," Katumpa answered with a very final note in his voice.

At about sunset one of the Baluba tribesmen came to us saying, "The Batua want to see you. Pastor Katumpa, they remember you from last year when you were here. They want you to come again."

"Both of us?" I asked, "or just Pastor Katumpa?"

"Both are to come," he said. "But you will have to promise not to 'scratch with the stick on the white bark.'"

"What does that mean, Katumpa?" I asked.

44

"State men scratch on white bark with a stick when they visit the Baluba villages. Then the villagers have to grow cotton, corn, and beans for the state men. The Batua pay taxes to no man."

We crossed the village to the Batua's hunting camp and I was very careful not to bring out any "white bark" or to "scratch with a stick." The fearsome little warriors were well armed with poison arrows and sharp knives.

"Do you see those big, strong, stupid Baluba?" the Batua chieftain said to me. "They look down on us, and think we are stupid. But they have to pay us to hunt for them while they work in fields like women to pay taxes to state men. We pay taxes to no man," he said with pride.

"Oh, I think you are a wonderful, courageous warrior," I said to the mean-looking little chieftain. "Your reputation for hunting skill and courage goes unequaled far and wide.[1] The Batua are unsurpassed in all these forests. If I had your courage I wouldn't have to pay taxes either."

He laughed at my weakness and said, "You hunt with a 'fire stick' because you are afraid. I hunt with my bow and arrows, because I am without fear."

"But are you not afraid to cross the Last River and to go into the Unknown Forest?" I asked.

"Everyone fears death," he said. "No one knows the other side."

From there we moved into a discussion of the "affair of God." I have never met a people more closed than these Batua. If they had any religion, they certainly were not going to share it with me. Finally, as the evening length-

---

1. The Pygmy reputation in the 1950s was awesome. They would kill lions with knives, attacking head-on. They expected to have some of their number killed, but the lion would die, no matter how many tribesmen died. Elephants too were killed with the Pygmies' simple weapons. One or two would attract the animal's attention while another came up behind and cut its hamstring. With the great tendon at the back of the hock cut, it could not run away and was limited in its defense against the attackers. Sometimes other elephants carry a wounded comrade between them for miles away from the scene of the battle. But the Batua simply move their hunting camp and follow until the kill is accomplished.

45

ened, I set up a battery-driven slide projector and screen. I showed a short film on the life, death, and resurrection of Christ. The Batua showed little interest in either the pictures or the story until we got to the crucifixion of Christ. Then pandemonium broke out. They danced, shouted, rolled on the ground, and laughed and laughed. They demanded I show the gruesome scene again and again. They were not remotely interested in either the burial or the resurrection; only the suffering and agonizing death appealed to them. It seemed to me impossible to communicate with them on any significant spiritual level.

When we finally gave up talking and rolled out our bedrolls, the chieftain indicated an open, grass-roofed shelter. "There you will sleep," he said decisively. Two young Batua girls appeared and stood before us, wearing the current clothing—a scanty skin breechcloth. "They will sleep with you," the leader announced with the pleasure of a good host.

Believe me, I thought and prayed quickly before I answered that command. Any wrong move now would end our lives, and we could easily offend these volatile people who were simply extending to us the hospitality of their culture.

"Courageous hunter," I said, "your gracious hospitality overwhelms us. We are honored to be invited to spend the night in your village. But I have a problem. Just as you have taboos among your people, we of the New Tribe who follow Jesus Christ as our Chieftain also have our taboos. It would break the taboos of my tribe to sleep with any woman who is not my wife. Therefore, we cannot accept your gracious offer."

Suddenly the pleasant scene grew ugly. Warriors began talking in angry tones and moved to encircle Katumpa and me. My companion was strangely silent, and I felt very much on my own in this one. "Lord, please help me say the right thing now, and please take care of Merry and the children," I prayed.

"No man sleeps alone in my camp," the leader said with

uncompromising finality. And a couple of warriors pulled out poison-tipped arrows, ready to arm their short bows.

"But great leader," I replied as calmly and confidently as I could, "you invited us to sit with you and to be your guests for the evening. We accepted your hospitality and have enjoyed talking with you very much. It is an honor to be able to get to know you and your people. I am confident a great chieftain would not insist that an invited guest in his village be forced to break a strong taboo of his culture. When you come to sit with me in my village, I will not try to force you to break your honored taboos. Such a thing would dishonor my leadership among my people. Allow us to follow our customs and to sleep alone in the shelter you have provided."

"You don't like our women," an angry warrior said in a threatening voice.

"Oh no," I lied. "Your young women are beautiful, and are worthy of only Batua warriors. Anything less would degrade them. Would you offer your best girls to a Belgian state man, or a white hunter who has to hunt with a 'fire stick?'" With this they laughed, and the crisis passed as suddenly as it had arisen.

"You will sleep alone in the shelter. If you move in the night, you will die," the leader announced. It was obvious he could not understand the ignorance of people with strange ways.

"Rest in peace all night, courageous hunter," I answered. "We will not move until the sun arises and the people come back to life." The two men who stood guard with poison arrows made sure we kept our promise.

The next day Katumpa was strangely silent. We traveled most of the day with very little conversation, each of us deep in thought. Finally I observed, "Katumpa, we were invited to sit with the Batua because they remembered you from last year when you visited there."

"That is correct," he said.

"I have been wondering why I had to go to such length

47

explaining the taboos of our tribe to them since you had visited them before."

"Some things I would rather not discuss with you," he said with finality in his voice.

The following year, after much prayer for the Batua, I found a young Christian man whose mother was Batua and who was willing to attempt sharing the gospel with the hunters. We gave him as much training as we could to equip him for the difficult and dangerous mission, then sent him off with much prayer. He got a good response among them while they were hunting for the Baluba. None, it is true, showed any desire to become followers of Christ or members of the New Tribe, but they were friendly and invited him to sit with them in their village. However, one night, as was the Batua custom, all the people moved silently into the forest. The evangelist, finding the village empty when he awoke, followed the tracks of the hunters into the deep forest. He was never heard of again.

Being different can be dangerous. When our customs clash with the prevailing, controlling culture, there is a price to be paid. And Christians, who are *in* this world but not *of* it, have no real choice between conformity and conflict. We are called to be different from non-Christians around us. We are commanded by Christ himself to live among them and to conduct our lives as living witnesses of a loving God to lost people.

> They think it strange that you do not plunge with them into the same flood of dissipation, and they heap abuse on you. But they will have to give account to him who is ready to judge the living and the dead (1 Peter 4:4-5).

It is the plan of God to distribute his followers throughout his world among people who do not know him or serve him. Through the lives and the words of his faithful followers God continues his gracious offer of life to those who repent of their sins, turn from their former lifestyle, and follow his teachings in the New Tribe. True, it is dangerous to be different. But the danger is well worth the cost, if one can cross life's last river with the quiet peace that Jesus will have someone there to meet you on the other side to lead you to the Village of God where you can sit with his people forever.

8

Prayer and Patience

I tell you the truth, my Father will give you whatever you ask in my name. Until now you have not asked for anything in my name. Ask and you will receive, and your joy will be complete (John 16:23-24).

Do you really believe that God answers the prayers of his followers?" I asked my friend. I was sitting in the church office of Pastor Mutombo David, a popular preacher and spiritual leader among the Baluba people of Africa's Congo.

"Look at my hand," said the humble man of God as he held it out in my direction. "It was once covered with leprosy. I prayed and God answered my prayers. I am sure God answers prayers that please his purposes for all his children."

The story of Mutombo David was well known among his people. The son of a chieftain of the Kalonji, Mutombo had been selected to study at the new mission station school at Bibanga. He and his colleagues were instructed to "learn the secrets of the whites and bring them back to the people of Kalonji."

Mutombo was a diligent student. He observed, he listened, and he learned. He compared the new ways and the new wisdom with the teachings of his tribe, and he became convinced that the true "secret of the whites" that made them powerful was the supernatural power of prayer to *Nzambi* (the Creator God) in the name of *Yesu Kilisto* (Jesus Christ, God's son). He became a follower of *Yesu* and a member of the New Tribe, and was given a Christian name—David—as was the custom of the time.

A Christian girl at the mission became his wife and the two continued their studies until David was prepared to become a pastor. He served with great power throughout his tribal area and among neighboring tribes as well. He rapidly became a noted preacher and a much-sought-after source of spiritual wisdom and power. He could talk with *Nzambi* and get answers to his prayers.

After several years of rural ministry, David was called to serve the large church on the mission station. At the height of his very popular ministry, he noticed a red spot on his right hand. It grew and he became concerned. His regular ministry included a large group of people camped near the mission who had advanced cases of leprosy. There was no cure in the 1940s for the dreaded disease, and patients were sent by the government to the camp to live out the rest of their days among the "living dead." Fearfully, David showed his hand to the mission doctor who, after thorough examination, reached a conclusion: He had leprosy. He would have to move to the Leper Camp for treatment.

"But I have a wife and children," David implored. "And my ministry, what will happen to God's work here?"

"You will have to leave everything in God's hands," the doctor replied. "In this decision you have no choice."

Mutombo David went into the forest. For seven days he fasted and prayed. When he returned at the end of the week, he went directly to the hospital to consult with the doctor. The red spot had disappeared, and his hand was completely healed: David was declared free of leprosy. He had talked with God and had received God's answer.

God continued to bless David's ministry and he continued to inspire great confidence in the power of prayer. After all, was not David a living example of answered prayer?

Soon after the miraculous answer to Mutombo David's prayer for healing, another very popular preacher among the Baluba experienced a similar problem. Mutombo Elijah was the son of a leader among the people of Kalambai. He, too, was selected to study at the mission to learn the "secrets of the whites." As a colleague and close friend of David, the two boys studied, worked, and played together, and made their profession of faith in Christ together.

Elijah also was called to serve God as an evangelist and preacher of the Good News among his people. He married a Christian girl and became the most powerful and tireless evangelist in the Lubilash Valley, known among the missionaries as the "Billy Sunday" or "Billy Graham" of the Baluba. It therefore came as a great shock to all the Christians to learn that Mutombo Elijah had leprosy.

Well aware of his friend David's answer to prayer, Elijah also went into the forest to pray. He stayed for one week and returned to the hospital for an examination.

"I am sorry, Elijah," said the doctor. "You will have to move to the Leper Camp for treatment."

"But my wife and my children and God's work—who will take care of them while I live with the 'living dead'?"

"God will look after his people, Elijah, and he will not forget you."

"Where you go, I go," Elijah's strong wife declared. "You are my husband. I am your wife. God will take care of me and our children. And if he allows us to get leprosy we will accept it from him. We go with you." And she did just that.

For fifteen years Elijah lived and worked with the "living dead." Before he and his wife moved into their community, the residents of the Leper Camp were noted for

53

drunkenness, fights, immorality, and even murder. But when the powerful preacher began to teach and lead them, they responded in large numbers and with open hearts, and the Leper Camp church became the largest congregation in the whole region.

Although the people lived on a survival stipend from the government, the offerings of the camp surpassed the contributions of the entire presbytery year after year. "We cannot be evangelists and tell other people about *Yesu*," they said, "so we must do what we can to send others and to pray for God's work." Each morning after prayers in the church at dawn, the entire camp moved into the "Lord's Acre" to work God's field before they worked their own. Some walked, some hobbled, a few crawled, but they all worked. Some had no hands because of advanced stages of leprosy, but all were grateful to be able to serve God.

Fifteen years after Pastor Elijah had contracted leprosy, the presbytery was holding a five-day meeting at which pastors and elders from twenty thousand square miles of towns and villages had gathered for prayer, fellowship, and annual planning. Because of his leprosy, Elijah never sat with us for the meeting, but remained with his people and accepted our decisions. But suddenly, in a moment that none of those gathered will ever forget, Elijah walked into the room and stood before us. He was wearing the white, flowing robe worn by leprous people to indicate their uncleanness; his burning eyes held us in anticipation as he greeted us in his strong, commanding voice:

"I have an announcement to make so you can share my joy and praise God with me. After fifteen years of prayer, God has answered my prayers. I am clean. My sickness has been arrested. I am free at last."

Great joy filled us all as we arose and praised God for his power and love. At length Pastor Mutombo David spoke.

"Brother Elijah, we are now making work assignments for the coming year. This is a new and wonderful year for all of us with your recovery. It would be an honor for me to pass the church I have been serving to you. Will you

54

accept it as the field you will now work?" David was, at that time, serving the most prestigious church in the presbytery—in the diamond mine at Bakawanga—and it was considered an honor to be the pastor for such a congregation.

Other pastors arose to make similar speeches, until the moderator ended the discussion by affirming, "Mutombo Elijah, you can choose any parish you want in the presbytery."

"Brothers," replied Elijah, "you do not understand. God had to lay a very heavy hand on me fifteen years ago to accept his assignment to live and serve him in the Leper Camp. Without the leprous mark, I would never have obeyed him. Throughout the years he has blessed me there. He has kept my wife and children clean. He has built up his church. He has answered much prayer. He has given me fullness of his joy, and I am grateful. Now you say, with all good intentions, 'Take your pick, Mutombo, of any church in the presbytery. All we have is yours.'

"Brothers, God makes the assignments. He owns the churches. Who will take my place in the camp? Will one of you become pastor of the flock I serve? No. I will stay where God has placed me until he moves me out to serve another people. I am grateful for your concern and for your generous love, but I will stay where God has placed me."

Eventually advances in modern medicine made treatment of leprosy possible in the villages. People with the disease could seek treatment at the mission hospital and were no longer forced by law to remain in the Leper Camp. They could return to their villages between treatments and were not forced to remain in isolation. By the end of our time among the Baluba people, the number of patients in the camp had diminished from over five hundred to less than one hundred; yet Pastor Mutombo Elijah and his wife remained to serve this dwindling flock of people whose cases were too advanced for them to return to their former homes.

What did Jesus mean when he said, "I tell you the truth, my Father will give you whatever you ask in my name. . . . Ask and you will receive, and your joy will be complete" (John 16:23-24)? Does God answer prayer? Does he answer all prayers offered in faith by his people? I believe he does. I believe that all prayers of Christians are answered by our loving heavenly Father who sees, knows, and cares. However, he is not bound by his promises to answer prayers just the way they are asked, nor is he bound by the asker's timetable. Mutombo David received an immediate answer to his prayer of faith, and he was healed. Mutombo Elijah accepted God's negative answer and worked for fifteen years before he was healed. God answered both men's prayers, and God's timing was perfect. Prayer and patience go together in God's plans for Mutombo David, for Mutombo Elijah, and for all of the members of the New Tribe.

9

The Lion and the Leopard

And what more shall I say? I do not have time to tell about Gideon, Barak, Samson, Jephthah, David, Samuel and the prophets, who through faith conquered kingdoms, administered justice, and gained what was promised; who shut the mouths of lions, quenched the fury of the flames, and escaped the edge of the sword; whose weakness was turned to strength; and who became powerful in battle and routed foreign armies (Heb. 11:32-34).

What does it take to 'shut the mouths of lions?' "
I asked my friend, Pastor Mutombo Elijah. We were surrounded by the Young Lions, as the military youth groups called themselves. Each night they encircled our homes and chanted their Communist-inspired slogans of revolution, liberation, and death to the enemies of their leaders. All night long they marched and sang. The hospital male nurses, who came at all hours to our home for medical instructions from my wife, Merry, were afraid to pass through the line of marching soldiers, but were allowed to come so that medical work could continue at the mis-

sion hospital. Not only were the homes of missionaries encircled, but also those of all the strong Christian leaders in the village. Some of our leaders had fled the mission and returned to their native villages. Those who remained were inspired to do so by the strong leadership of Pastor Elijah.

"What does it take to stop the mouths of lions?" Elijah replied. "It takes a leopard like me, who has faith in God."

Among the Baluba people of Africa's Congo, the lion is the "king of beasts," feared for his awesome strength and vicious courage. But the leopard is the real king; he fears neither lions nor any other beast that roams the grasslands. Kings in the Congo wear leopard skins as a sign of their royal power, and fearful subjects are forced to sit on a leopard skin when honest witness is demanded. (To lie would incur the wrath of the leopard.) Any part of this animal has great value in native charms and medicine.

"We are leopards of the Lord," continued Elijah. "We have nothing to fear of those young lions who chant in the night to keep their courage up."

"Does our presence among you add to your danger?" I asked, because other pastors had ceased to travel with me for fear of becoming involved in my difficulties with revolutionaries.

"Certainly," came the strong, honest reply. "These people are against all Christians who stand up for what they believe. But don't let that concern you, my brother. We will fight the devil together. And, if we are killed, we will go together into the presence of our King. We are leopards. Who are we to fear young lions?"

And Elijah was not afraid.

Confusion and Communism usually go hand in hand, and the Belgian Congo was no exception during the troubled days of 1959 and 1960. Young men had been captured by Russian agents in Congo both before and during World War II. After years of training in revolutionary tactics in Russia, they were sent back to the Congo to establish Communist cells in all the principal centers of the colony.

58

"If all this is known, why have you not stamped out those centers and neutralized the leaders?" I asked an important Belgian leader. His reply surprised me.

"We have not outlawed the Communist Party in Belgium, nor here in the Congo. And besides, the colony is not paying enough return on our investments here to warrant fighting for it. We are going to let them have it."

During the early days of the Congo independence chaos, the missionaries who were not from Belgium were, for the most part, appreciated and protected. When intertribal wars raged around us, our mission trucks ran loads of human cargo between the Baluba and the Lulua areas. We tied the covers down and lied at road blocks. "What are you hauling?" the soldiers would ask, "*banto* or *binto* [people or things]?" Hundreds of lives were saved by helping people get back among their own tribes when senseless slaughter was the order of the day. And, after all, "*banto*" and "*binto*" sound a lot alike under pressure.

When the Belgian government relinquished control, localized intertribal warfare became pandemonium. African troops murdered their Belgian officers, and fought and plundered their way across the country in a wild attempt to reach the safety of their native tribal areas. Women were raped while husbands and children watched. Men were beaten and many of them killed. Property was stolen or destroyed. We sat by our radio, listening as day after day still more cities were added to the list of destruction.

Word came from my Belgian friend who commanded the garrison at Kabinda (a state post some fifty miles east of us): "Evacuate at once. Troops are headed your way." A well-ordered high command had determined the schedule and established the methods best designed to rid the Congo of all non-Communist whites, regardless of their mission in the land. Other nations were advising their citizens to flee, but the U.S. Consulate saw no danger.

The five missionary families in residence at Bibanga had no desire to add to the danger for Congolese Christian leaders who would carry on the work, so we followed our prearranged plans. We left in a five-car convoy at three in the morning, our cars packed for a five-day trip to the country's southern border. On our way past the Roman Catholic mission at Katanda, we stopped to pick up five Catholic sisters and their Mother Superior. At first the Mother Superior refused to go or to allow her sisters to leave with us, but when I gave her no choice, she smiled and said, "Since we have no choice, sisters, let's go quickly," and they moved out with us into the unknown darkness.

At the Lublish River our convoy would have to cross on a motor-driven ferry. I entered the village calling for the *Capita* (head man) Kasonga. He was an old friend of mine and of the mission. As a professional hunter, I had killed wild game that threatened the people of his village. At his request, I had killed the crocodile which hunted at his crossing. A big bull hippopotamus had killed several people and destroyed their canoe, so I killed him for my friend Kasonga and his people. With more than eighty hippopotamuses grazing near the fields of the village, I had frequently helped move them upstream and had left tons of meat for my friends. So, I was sure Kasonga would help us.

I was mistaken.

"If we allow you to pass, *Muambi* [Preacher], the Young Lions will come, burn our village, and kill us," Kasonga explained.

We were left with the choice of shooting our way across or turning back to face well-armed, drunken troops. "If we fight our way through," the other men observed, "we will have nothing to come back to." Their wisdom outweighed my desire to go on, so we returned to the mission. Before leaving Kasonga's village, I prayed, "Heavenly Father, please judge between Kasonga and his village and your people who have served them." Little did I dream that God would judge so harshly. The Young Lions came in the night, burned the village and murdered most of the villagers, even though they had obeyed their orders not to help us.

60

We arrived back at the mission around daylight. I was too tired to think, so I went to bed and slept soundly until a small plane flew over our house. The pilot dropped an object in our yard and then disappeared into the nearby valley. I picked up a new copy of *Time Magazine*. "I appreciate the airmail delivery, John," I muttered, "but right now I couldn't care less about *Time*." But I discovered that the magazine contained a note: "Get the women and children to the airfield at once. Bring only people. No baggage."

In a few minutes we were at the airstrip with women and children. John Davis, a former U.S. combat pilot, landed, picked up our loved ones, and was airborne before a crowd could gather. Much relieved, my colleague Frank Vandegrift and I returned to our houses to rest and make plans. We advised the local chieftain to fell trees across our road so the soldiers would have to walk in the high grass to get to us. Several kilometers of big trees laying in their path did encourage the soldiers to pass our mission station without plunder.

Little did we know that our wives and children were under siege in the city of Luluabourg. Belgian farmers and businessmen with hunting guns fought off well-armed Congolese soldiers until Belgian paratroopers could be flown in to rescue our people and secure the airport. Frank called on his short-wave radio for help, and received confirmation from a U.S. Navy plane en route to Italy that an Air Force plane was on its way to Luluabourg to rescue U.S. citizens. The next day we talked by short-wave with the pilot of the American plane as he flew over our station on his way out of Congo. He assured us that our wives and children were safe on board. We were truly grateful. Merry was eight months pregnant with our fifth child at the time and that kind of activity was not exactly what a doctor would have prescribed.

Several days after the evacuation of our families, John Davis returned to fly Frank and me to safety. Pastor Elijah and a truckload of Christians from a leper camp accompanied us as we drove to the landing strip. When we arrived, these Christians quickly surrounded us, pressing close upon us. Some kept looking across the field toward a nearby village, so I asked Elijah what they were looking for.

"There are men in that village with guns and they have been told to stop your escape. We have come to protect you. To kill you, they will have to kill us as well."

The words of Jesus came to my mind as we stood there, surrounded by leper-camp Christians who shielded us from death with their own bodies: "Greater love has no one than this, that one lay down his life for his friends" (John 15:13). Truly we stood among friends that day.

"I know you must go, *Kalambai*," Mutombo Elijah said with deep feeling. "Your country has called you and you must go. But come back, and we will fight the lions together. Leopards like us have nothing to fear from lions."

> Let us fix our eyes on Jesus, the author and perfecter of our faith. . . . Consider him who endured such opposition from sinful men, so that you will not grow weary and lose heart (Heb. 12:2-3).

10

The Man in the Leather Hat

My sheep listen to my voice; I know them, and they
follow me. I give them eternal life, and they shall never
perish; no one can snatch them out of my hand. My
Father, who has given them to me, is greater than all;
no one can snatch them out of my Father's hand. I and
the Father are one (John 10:27-30).

A cool evening breeze moves gently across the
central square of the quiet Brazilian town called Colinas.
After a hot day traveling in north Goias to reach my
destination, it feels good to be resting on a park bench surrounded by green grass and flowers, watching the children
play as soft lights blink on around the town square. Down
the street the doors of the church are opened, lights come
on inside, and music from a little pump organ drifts across
the evening stillness.

Sitting here in quiet Colinas, my mind fills with
memories of the days when the city was a tough and
dangerous cow town on the northern frontier of Brazil's
expansion into the largely uninhabited interior. When the
Brasilia-Belém Highway was being cut through the newly-
opened Indian lands in the early sixties, construction was

63

halted at Colinas for a long time. Sixty miles of deep, loose sand was making road building very difficult and costly and the trail northward was becoming a graveyard for trucks and jeeps. The old name for Colinas on early flight charts was *Vamos Ver* ("We shall see"). On the northern side of the sand, the first village was called *Vieu* ("Now you see").

When construction was held up on this highway, those who accompanied the construction crews—prostitutes,[1] gamblers, and frontier businessmen—usually remained among the unemployed workers waiting for better days. Frequently, criminals wanted for crimes in other places also congregated at the end of the line. Colinas was such a town when we first arrived to plant a church. The Communist mayor with his supporting gunmen did little to make the village a nice place in which to live and raise a family.

Now, twelve years after our early church-planting efforts in Colinas, I rest in the park and recall experiences and people God has used to change this town. Those experiences have changed *my* life as well and they are memories I will never forget. Why, the old Snubbing Post used to be right here where I'm sitting. . . .

As I stood there in the dusty town square with my back to the Snubbing Post, a violin in my hand and a gun in my face, I would have rather been just about any place else in the world.

1. One time five prostitutes stopped me at the airstrip in Colinas to ask me to sterilize them. They said babies were hard on their business. I assured them I was not in that kind of business, but said I would be delighted to see all of them in church that night. Some did come, but others continued their nightly activities. I later found out that the leading Communist newspaper in the state of Goias had run an article on American Presbyterian missionaries working in north Goias. The article accused us of distributing among the peoples of the Amazon basin powdered milk that would make them sterile. The sinister objective of the Americans, said the article, was to depopulate the great Amazon basin so that the United States could invade and take it over. It took fervent speeches from friendly senators and a thorough investigation of our work by federal police to clear us of these Communist charges.

We had arrived in Colinas early in the morning—Jose, Benjamin, and I—and had walked through the town and visited every house and business, inviting everyone to a meeting we were planning for that night at the Snubbing Post. (The Snubbing Post was a large log sunk deep into the ground and used by cowboys with wild horses; they would tie their broncos close to it for easier mounting—a process made even more difficult when the rider was half drunk. The Post was also a much-used public utility, serving upon occasion as the town jail. Prisoners were secured to it for a night and a day, then released or shot. The Post also served as the town newspaper, with notices of public interest being posted there.)

When we had asked the Communist mayor for permission to hold our meeting in the square, he had replied, "Certainly."

"Will you also come?" we asked. "It would be an honor to have you attend."

"I am too busy."

"Mr. Mayor," I continued, "sometimes the boys who have had too much to drink cause some trouble and make a lot of noise. Sometimes they shoot too low. Could you give us some police to help keep order tonight?"

The knife-scarred lip of the mayor curled in a cruel grin and he answered, "If your God cannot protect you, why should I?" He did have a point there, but I did not appreciate his logic.

When evening began to fall and shadows lengthened, lamps began to flicker in the bars that surrounded the square. Children played soccer in the sand near the Post, and I leaned against it to begin my part of the program. I played my violin—softly at first, then with more vigor and a little more noise. One violin is not much competition for the noisy loudspeakers that would soon begin to batter the evening stillness from the bars and gambling halls.

The ballplayers gathered with interest at the Post.

65

"What's going on?" the children asked.

"We have come to give you a great program," said Jose. "We have come to tell you wonderful things tonight, and you will want to hear it all." He got the children singing Christian songs while I played and played.

Shadows lengthened and darkness fell rapidly on the square. Mothers, concerned about their children being out after dark, came to see and most of them stayed. Drinkers in the bars saw women in the street and came at once to look and comment. As the Lord hung his full moon in the sky, bringing soft light to the town square, a motley crowd of some two hundred people gathered at the Snubbing Post to hear and to see.

Using his beautiful voice and warm personality, Jose soon had the crowd singing and laughing and feeling at home with us. A knife fighter before his conversion to Christ, he knew how to talk with these people. During the singing he gave his testimony, sharing how he had become a Christian and telling of the good things that had followed his decision to surrender his life to God.

Benjamin, a 220-pound former street fighter from the city of Sao Paulo, spoke God's message with beauty, power, and sincerity. He had been a Communist before coming to Christ, and his job in the Party had been to instigate riots in city parks. He also had been active in Communist-led labor unions, and he knew his way around the rough side of life.

Throughout the service, with the circle of children pressing us close to the Post, my attention had been fixed on the hard countenance of a scar-faced, bearded man with a leather hat pulled low over his forehead. His cold, cruel eyes seemed fixed in my direction, causing me great discomfort. My job that evening was to invite anyone interested in becoming a Christian to come forward for special prayer and additional information. When I gave God's invitation that night, the first to move forward was the man in the leather hat. The crowd parted, the children made way for him to pass, and he stood before me in grim, threatening silence. The crowd was quiet and my colleagues were not within my sight. I felt very much alone.

The man's hand moved smoothly into his shirt and came out with a large revolver which he held steadily trained on me. I thought about any possible moves I could make. The violin in my hand might look good on his head, but any bullet fired at so close a range would not be likely to miss the target. So I prayed. And as I did I looked into the cold eyes beneath the leather hat and waited for him to make the next move. The words he then spoke became fixed in my memory for life.

"Preacher, see this gun?"

"*Sim, Senhor* [Yes, Mister]." I wondered how he thought I could see anything else.

"This gun has gotten me everything I have ever had in life. Without it I am nothing. But I like what I have heard tonight. I'm giving you my gun and want you to sell it and use the money toward building a church here in Colinas. It is not much, but it is all I have." And with these simple words, he handed his gun to me.

"Neighbor," I answered, "God will take your gun and use the money for his glory, but he wants more than that from you." I could talk more easily with his gun in my hand.

"That is all I have to give. And without it, I can't stay here. There are too many people who would like to catch me without it. I'll be gone by morning, Preacher, and you will not see me again."

"God wants your life, not just your gun, *Senhor*. He wants you to repent of the bad things you have done in life and to follow his teachings. He wants you to become a member of the church you want to help build here."

Wistfully he replied, "I'll have to move on, Preacher. I can't stay here without a gun."

The next morning he was gone and was never seen around Colinas again.

... The soft, fluorescent street lamps lighting

up the square are not at all like the full moon that lit the dusty square twelve years ago, but then, everything around here has changed. The prostitutes and gamblers have moved on or changed their professions. The bars are quiet places now, much more respectable than they used to be. The loudspeakers today play very different music than before and are often used to play Christian songs and invite the people to church.

Most of the fifteen adults who stood with us at the Snubbing Post to confess Christ twelve years ago are still here, serving as leaders in the church and in the community. But I still wonder what happened to the scar-faced gunman in the leather hat. "I want other people to hear what I have heard tonight," he had said. "I want a church built here so God's work will go on and on."

There are several churches in Colinas today, but the first got its start when a lonely gunman gave up his gun. I often wonder how much that gift cost him. It cost him his *way* of life, that's for sure. Did it cost him his *life* as well?

As I looked out over the crowd at the Snubbing Post that night long ago, I would never have selected the man in the leather hat to become a Christian. His response to the voice of Jesus through Jose and Benjamin and me taught me that Jesus truly does call his own sheep. His undershepherds are commanded to witness, to invite, and to urge all people to follow the Good Shepherd; but it is Christ who makes the Christian.

I give them eternal life, and they shall never perish; no one can snatch them out of my hand (John 10:28).

11

Maria of Paradise

I have other sheep that are not of this sheep pen. I must bring them also. They too will listen to my voice, and there shall be one flock and one shepherd (John 10:16).

My first encounter with Maria was on a narrow street in Paradise, a wild Brazilian frontier town that exploded into existence when road construction crews were held up by an extended rainy season. Gun battles, knife fights, and barroom brawls left people dead in the streets at least once a week, while the small group of soldiers who tried to police the town had to be replaced about once every month. (Many citizens of Paradise either had reason to dislike the law or thought the soldiers were involved in much of the crime. On at least three occasions, townspeople shot at the soldiers, killing several of them.) There were also fourteen houses of vice in the town, all of them teeming with activity.

Walking with evangelist-teacher Jose Siqueira one evening, I saw a woman coming toward us who carried herself in the way that marks women of her profession. When we passed in the narrow street, I greeted her.

"*Boa tarde, Dona* [Good evening, Madam]."

"*Boa tarde, Senhor*," she replied and continued on her way.

"Do you know that woman, Reverend?" Jose questioned.

"*What* she is, is obvious. *Who* she is, I do not know."

"That is Maria of Paradise, Pastor."

"Should I know her?"

"She knows you and has been trying to hire gunmen to shoot you and Reverend Camenisch."

"That does make her more interesting, Jose. What is her problem with us?"

"The city fathers have told her she must move her public house to another part of town. They say it is not right to have that kind of thing going on across the street from a church. She thinks it must be one of you who denounced her."

"It does sound like a good idea, Jose, but neither of us has tried to move her out. Why has she had problems finding gunmen to shoot us?"

"She is offering only fifteen dollars for each of you."

"But the going rate around here these days is about five dollars, and several kill because they enjoy it."

"Yes, but they all want fifty dollars to kill an American."

"I'm flattered, but not pleased," I answered, determined not to walk around alone in Paradise anymore.

My second encounter with Maria of Paradise came at the end of a thirty-four mile ride. My grey stallion walked by the new church without even lifting his head, but when he came to Maria's house, he turned in and stopped at the hitching rail. Maria and several of her girls were sitting on the porch when my pagan horse turned in. Maria laughed and the girls giggled.

"*Boa tarde, Dona*," I said with a rather sick grin. "It looks like someone has been riding my horse."

70

"Won't you come in, Reverend?" Maria invited.

"No thank you, *Dona*. I just stopped by to invite you and all the girls to church. We have a great service planned for this evening—with imported music and imported preaching. (I didn't tell her I was both.) We would appreciate your coming, and I'm sure you will like it if you come."

Maria laughed a hard, cold laugh and said, "Some day, perhaps."

I tipped my hat and rode away, conscious of the fact that my back was turned on the woman who wanted me shot.

On a visit to Paradise two months later I was eating supper with Jose and Dr. Joe Wilding, a well-known Brazilian doctor, when our meal was suddenly interrupted.

"Dr. Joe—come quickly!" someone shouted. "One of Maria's girls has set herself on fire!"

Joe and I ran to Maria's house and entered a small, dingy room where we found a thirteen-year-old Indian girl dying of self-inflicted burns.

"Why has she done this?" Joe asked Maria.

"Her father put her out on her own—too many mouths to feed. A truck driver picked her up and used her until he got here. He kicked her out on the street, and I took her in. Today she said to one of the girls, 'I'm going to burn the hell out of my life.' She drank a large cup of kerosene, poured the rest on her chest, and set herself on fire."

As Dr. Joe did what he could to save the girl's life, I stood by the bed. When he was finished he said to me, "I have done all I can do. Now you pray."

Down the hall in the sitting room a needlepoint tapestry had attracted my attention. I said to Maria and the girls looking on, "Your tapestry in there says 'Jesus is here.' If he is really here, we will pray to him. Only he can help this girl now." And as I led in prayer I had confidence that he was listening. I prayed for the Indian girl, for Maria, and for all the girls who worked in her house.

Several months later I was again in Paradise. This time we really *did* have imported music and an imported preacher—we were inaugurating the new church building with a four-day series of meetings. I went by Maria's house to invite her to the services.

"*Dona* Maria, Dr. Joe and I came to your house when you called us. Now I am inviting you and your girls to the house of God. Will you come?"

"Do you mean you would let me into your church?" she asked.

"I don't have a church, *Dona*. It is God's house and he lets all of us sinners come into his house. That is the only place where people like us can find hope and help."

"But the other people—they will not let me in," she said.

"Be my guest," I answered. "You and the girls are invited."

It was my custom before a Paradise church service to collect at the door all the revolvers, shotguns, and any knives people would give up. This arsenal was kept safe behind locked doors until needed by our people walking home in the dark streets. I prefer to preach to a disarmed congregation, and even the soldiers who came were forced to cooperate.

I was busy stacking guns on my cot in a room near the front door of the church when I heard loud talking outside. The loud, harsh voice of Maria rose above the others: "What do you mean, I can't come in here? When you come to my house I don't turn you away."

When I stepped out I found Maria confronted by a man I was training to be an elder. He seemed embarrassed, but determined.

"What's the trouble?" I asked.

"Maria wants to come into church," the provisional elder answered.

"Why not? I invited her. She is my guest."

"You would let her come into church like that?" the man answered, and I looked at Maria. Those were the days of

72

the miniskirt, and Maria had outdone the style. Her dress was too low on top and too short on the bottom, and there was much too much of Maria in between. What do you say at a time like that?

"She can't come to church with a dress like that," the provisional elder said forcefully.

"Do you want me to ask her to take it off?" I asked. Everyone around us laughed and Maria walked down the aisle with that "professional" way she had of calling attention to herself. She sat near the front and everyone in the church was aware of her presence and cheap perfume.

During the service Maria pulled up on her low-cut dress, then, seeing she lost too much on the bottom, pulled it down again. I don't think she was very comfortable in church that evening. But the next night she was there again, and this time she had five of her girls with her. (Among them was the little Indian girl who had set herself on fire. Certainly God had answered us that night when we prayed for her.) Maria and the girls wore dresses that caused no problems at the door. On the last night of the four-night series, I gave an invitation and Maria with her five girls joined the group at the front of the church to confess Christ. When she stood beside the communion table, tear tracks marking her painted face, she asked, "Pastor, do you think God will accept a woman like me?"

"Jesus died for people like you and me, Maria," I answered. "He will take us like we are, but will not let us stay like that. He has much better things in store for people who love him and follow him."

There were sixty new Christians in the communicant class at Paradise after our inauguration services. Maria and the girls were among them. That was certainly the most honest communicant class I ever taught in cowboy country; whenever people talked better than they acted, Maria's laugh would bring them back to reality.

After six months in the class and regular attendance in church, Sunday school, and prayer meeting, it was time for those who had made professions of faith to become members of the church. Maria came to the elders and me and announced that it was also time for her to take the girls someplace where none of them were known. "We need to make a new start in a new place so we can live like Christians," she explained. "We will join the church where God leads us."

Before Maria left with her girls I asked her, "Did you ever find out who talked with the city fathers and had your business moved away from the church? I know it was neither my colleague nor I."

"Yes, Pastor, it was that rascally priest, and he was one of our regular customers."

I never heard of Maria again, but I trust she and her girls have continued to follow the One who laid down his life for the "other sheep."

The next time I was in Paradise I missed having Maria and the girls in the service, but I was glad they were able to go away and seek a new life. And, as I soon discovered, I was not the only one who was thinking about them that evening. A hard-case cowboy had gotten past the men who were collecting and stacking weapons at the door of the church. I knew he had passed them by because he was still wearing his heavy spurs which clanked down on our concrete floor and left their marks on the paint. Beneath his dirty shirt was a bulge that looked a lot like a revolver. During the service he fixed his eyes on me; after the service he remained sitting while everyone else went out. Jose turned out the lamps and left me with only a little kerosene candle and a hard-case cowboy whose looks I did not like at all.

"Do you want to talk with me, neighbor?" I asked with some reluctance. His answer will go with me for life.

"*Sim, Senhor* [Yes, Mister]. I hear what you have said here tonight, and I like it. You said that a sinner like me can find forgiveness with God through Jesus Christ. That really is good news. I hear you, and I like it. I look around me and I believe it."

74

"What do you mean, *Senhor?*" I questioned.

"Did you see Antonio here tonight?"

"Yes, I know Antonio well."

"He used to be the most dishonest storekeeper in this town. Six months ago he got religion in this church, and has turned honest. I never thought it could happen. Then Black John, did you see him here?"

"Yes, John sang for us tonight and gave his testimony."

"I have known John for years, *Senhor.* There was not a meaner or more dangerous man in town than old John. Every time he drank, and he drank all the time, he looked for a fight. Since he got religion here, he neither drinks nor fights. If it could happen to John, I thought it might happen to me.

"But, *Senhor,* the ones who make me know what you say is true are Maria and those girls of hers. If God can make a Christian out of Maria, there is hope for me. I want to be a Christian like that too."

We know that Jesus is concerned for those "other sheep" who are not in the fold. As his under-shepherds we must share his concern, doing what we can to find those lost sheep. But there are significant questions we must consider if we truly wish to serve and follow the Good Shepherd.

What do those "other sheep" look like? They look like Maria and her girls, like Antonio and Black John, like the hard-case cowboy and the rest of the lost people of Paradise.

Where can they be found? They can be found almost anywhere but in the church and in close Christian circles. And they are not likely to push their way into Christian groups where they are not sure of their welcome.

How can they be reached? That is a more difficult question, because there is no standard pattern. All people are different. But the general way to find lost sheep and bring them to Christ is to go where they are, experience something of their lostness with them, and honestly share with them our hope and faith in Christ.

Are they really lost? Jesus said they are lost, and he laid down his life for them.

How far are we willing to go to reach them? That is for each of us who follow Christ to answer, and the measure of our love will be evaluated when we stand before our God.

> I lay down my life for the sheep. I have other sheep that are not of this sheep pen. I must bring them also (John 10:15b-16a).

12

Back of the Rim Rock
at Little Albert's

If you remain in me and my words remain in you, ask
whatever you wish, and it will be given you. This is to
my Father's glory, that you bear much fruit, showing
yourselves to be my disciples (John 15:7-8).

Out back of the rim rock that towered above the
town of Paradise a big Brazilian *festa* (feast) was planned
at the homestead of Little Albert. Taking off from my home
in Ceres at daylight, I piloted my small, single-engine
airplane for three hours through the rain to make what
normally was a two-hour flight. Jose met me at the airstrip
and I could tell something was not quite right.

"I didn't think you could come in the rain, Pastor."

"A *festa* at Little Albert's is worth the extra effort, Jose.
How soon can we be ready to ride?"

"It may take a little time, *Senhor*. We turned your horse
out in the big pasture because we didn't expect you in the
rain."

That indeed was big trouble. My trail horse in that

region was a thoroughly pagan stallion who could be caught for work only when cornered. When turned out in the big pasture, he considered it his day. We got the boys from the primary school to help crowd the unwilling horse close enough for me to rope him, and it was a hot high noon when we finally crossed the rim rock above Paradise. The rain ended and the temperature rapidly passed 105 dry degrees—and we still had thirty-four miles to ride to Little Albert's. Only the expectation of a large crowd of neglected people gathering at the homestead for the festivities encouraged me to push on. I love to preach and I especially enjoy preaching and discussing the gospel among lonely, neglected people. (Of course, the prospects of roasted venison and wild hog added to my anticipation.)

It was growing dark when we finally crossed the last ridge and looked into Little Albert's valley. The tiny homestead looked deserted. I saw no horses tied around the corral, no smoke of roasting meat, no sign of activity at all.

"It looks like they were not expecting us, *Senhor*. Perhaps it was the rain," Jose said.

When we rode into the yard, Little Albert met us at the door. "*Boa tarde, Senhores* [Good evening, Sirs]. Dismount and sit. We will have supper for you soon."

"Little Albert, where are all the people you promised? What has happened to the *festa*?"

"Oh *Senhor*, God sent the rain, and I did not think you would be able to fly in the rain. I told the neighbors not to come, but to wait for another time."

It had been a long, difficult flight, a hard chase to catch my horse, and a long, hot ride of more than thirty miles. A *festa* would have been well worth the effort, but now the burden of our excursion settled heavily on Jose and me. After bathing our horses and ourselves in a nearby stream, we rested in hammocks in the dirt-floored living room. A squealing pig ran from the kitchen and bumped my hammock on his way to safety.

"What did he say to you, *Senhor*?" Jose joked.

"I think he said we were stealing his supper," I said,

but when our cold, sand-filled beans and rice arrived, I wondered why the pig had made so much fuss. It takes time to heat up leftover food on a wood fire which has gone out, and Little Albert's six small children normally leave very little of whatever is cooked.

I was asked to lead family devotions that night. Jose sang and was bright and happy, and everyone responded to his cheer. I tried to fake it, but was not very successful. About halfway through the brief devotional, someone rode into the moonlit yard and hailed the house. Little Albert stepped out and soon returned with a lean, tall cowboy wearing homespun pants and shirt, with rusty spurs riding on his big, bare feet. After introductions, the cowboy squatted on a pack saddle in the corner of the living room, and I came to life. Now I understood why God had led me to push on to Little Albert's today. He had brought me to preach to this man. Little Albert, his wife, and all six of his children were professing Christians, so this man looked like the best I would get today, so I gave him the best I had. When I finished a short, clear presentation of God's gospel, I ended with an invitation. The man just sat there and looked at me. After a little urging I gave up, closed with prayer, and went out to check the hobbles on my stallion. I added a choke rope to be sure I would not have to walk out next morning. My pagan horse had run wild and was very romantic on the open range.

When I finished working on my horse, I became aware of someone standing near me.

"*Senhor*," the cowboy said, "I got the idea you wanted me to do something in there."

"That's right, neighbor. I surely did."

"What was it you wanted me to do?"

"I wanted you to become a Christian."

"All my life I have wanted to be a Christian, but nobody ever showed me how."

"Neighbor, I have just spent forty-five minutes of my life trying to tell you how to become a Christian."

"I still don't understand. Can you help me, *Senhor*?"

79

"No. I can't help you. I have done the best I can. But I know someone who can help."

"Who is that, *Senhor*?" the cowboy answered wistfully.

"The One who helped me become a Christian."

The tall cowboy and I knelt in the dust by the corral gate and I prayed, "Lord, I have tried to tell this man how to become a Christian, but he still does not understand. Will you please help him?" Then I said to the cowboy, "Talk to him. He is listening."

I have heard many prayers in my life, but never one quite like the prayer of that barefoot cowboy in a moonlit corral out back of the rim rock at Little Albert's.

"*Senhor Deus* [God, Sir], I am not much. I can neither read nor write. But I give you all I am and all I have, if you will have me."

I believe that humble prayer made it to the throne of grace as directly as any prayer I have ever heard. An hour later, with a new Bible and hymn book in his saddlebags, the cowboy rode out of the moonlit yard, heading home.

"Won't you spend the night?" Little Albert urged him. (It was past midnight.)

"No. I am a Christian now, and I can't wait to tell my wife and children." He rode away singing a new Christian chorus, and I prayed, "Lord, there he goes. He is not much, but he has offered you all he is and all he has if you will have him. Will you take him?"

Each week for six months the cowboy neighbor rode the ten miles to Little Albert's for Christian teaching and to learn a new hymn. He still could neither read nor write, but he could memorize, and that he did. He began gathering his neighbors at his homestead to share with them what he had learned and experienced. He would have someone else read a passage in the Bible and would then explain its meaning just as Little Albert had explained it to him. Each week he taught his group a new hymn as well.

According to Little Albert, the cowboy's group had grown to about forty-five people in six months. After about one year, they were well enough trained to go without the cowboy's leadership. He moved to another lonely region, began another homestead, and opened a new work. After about three years in the second location, the homespun cowboy with the big, bare feet and rusty spurs had a new group of new Christians meeting in his humble homestead. The last I heard of him through Little Albert, the man had moved again with his family and had started another new work.

"Lord, I am not much," he had prayed that night. "But I give you all I am and all I have if you will have me."

And I prayed when I heard the latest report about the homespun cowboy: "Lord, you don't need much to work with, do you? Just all we are and all we have."

> You did not choose me, but I chose you to go and bear *fruit—fruit* that will last. Then the Father will give you whatever you ask in my name (John 15:16, italics added).

13

Where the Girls Are Called Maria

He said to them, "Let the little children come to me, and do not hinder them, for the kingdom of God belongs to such as these. I tell you the truth, anyone who will not receive the kingdom of God like a little child will never enter it." And he took the children in his arms, put his hands on them and blessed them (Mark 10:14-16).

Electric lights were not the norm in New Glory during the 1960s, so these new ones lighting up the just-completed church building attracted some attention as they shone through the open windows. After starting up the generator that fed them, I stepped into the town square to look with pride at their warm glow. As I stood there in the dark, a big-eyed little Indian girl spoke to me with an awed and reverent voice.

"Isn't it beautiful, *Senhor*?" she said.

"It is beautiful, Maria," I replied.

"How did you know my name, *Senhor*?" she asked. Since almost all the girls in Brazil are Maria Something-or-other, my guess was easy. (Most of the boys there are Jose Something-or-other.)

"You look pretty enough to be Maria," I answered, and

then invited her to come with me to church—an inauguration service was scheduled to begin shortly.

"Oh *Senhor*, my dress is dirty and I have no shoes. I could not go into that church like this."

"You are beautiful, Maria, and no one needs shoes to come into God's house."

"I'll have to ask my father," she answered, excitement in her voice.

"Would you like for me to come with you to ask your father?"

"Oh no, *Senhor*," she said. "*Meu pai e muito perigoso* [my father is very dangerous]." In that country of dangerous men, very few attained the level of *muito perigoso*. I was impressed. I also noted the fear in the girl's voice at the thought of me going with her. As she ran off in the darkness to ask her "very dangerous" father if she could come to church, I prayed, "Lord, isn't that asking a lot of a little child?"

The opening service of our inauguration series was well under way when I saw little Maria come into the church with a clean dress, clean face, and clean, bare feet. At the close of the service, I gave an invitation for anyone wanting to become a Christian to come forward for special prayer and to enroll in a Bible study class. Maria was among the first to come down the aisle.

"*Senhor*," she asked, "may I be a Christian and belong to this church?"

"Yes, Maria," I answered, "but you will have to have your father's permission. Do you think he will let you come here?"

"I will ask him, *Senhor*."

"Would you like for me to come with you to ask him?"

Once again she answered, "Oh no, *Senhor*. My father is very dangerous."

Thinking that perhaps her father just did not like North Americans, I asked, "Would you like for someone from this church who lives here to go with you to talk with your father?"

84

"No, no, *Senhor*. He does not want to talk with anyone."

"Then, Maria, please tell your father that you want to be a Christian and belong to this church. Tell him we believe the Bible is the Word of God, and that we are in favor of God and against no one. And tell him I am giving him a special invitation to visit us here. It would be an honor for me to have him visit the church tomorrow night as my special guest."

"I will tell him, *Senhor*," she answered. After special prayer for Maria and for the others who had come forward with her, the barefoot little girl ran out of the church into the dark, dusty streets of New Glory.

The next evening Maria was the first to arrive when the lights came on. And with her was a little brother who rode the hip of his sister in the fashion typical of that place and time. She had to lean far to the side to balance his weight, but she had probably been carrying him all his life while her mother worked in the field and home.

"Good evening, Maria," I greeted. "I am glad you brought your brother, Jose."

"How did you know his name, *Senhor*?" Maria asked.

"Oh, he just looks like Jose, and besides, Maria should have a Jose with her, shouldn't she?"

That little boy looked like trouble in church to me, but his sister did a good job of keeping him reasonably quiet and in one place. When the invitation was given, Maria walked quickly down the aisle, again carrying her brother on her hip.

"Why have you come forward tonight, Maria?" I asked.

"I want Jose to be a Christian too."

I will confess Jose did not look like very good Christian material to me, but we prayed for him and enrolled him in a Sunday school class and I gave his name to one of our best Sunday school teachers. (The best ones spent time during the week visiting the families of their pupils, and I had a feeling Jose would need all the help he could get.)

85

"Did you give your father my special invitation to visit church?" I asked Maria.

"Yes, *Senhor*, but he did not say anything."

"Then ask him again to come. I would like to talk with him," I said. But I wondered if I really meant it.

As the lights came on in the church the next evening, Maria—with Jose on her hip—was again the first person in church. With her was a tall, fine-looking Indian woman with long black hair and a sad face. Her big black eyes never wavered from the preacher as he spoke with power, applying God's message to life's problems. When the invitation was given at the close of the service, little Maria came down the aisle—with Jose on her hip—leading her mother by the hand.

"My mother wants to be a Christian too," Maria said, with a bright, happy face.

There were many questions I would have liked to have asked this sad-faced woman, but in that country at that time it was better not to ask too many questions about a person's past.

"*Dona* Maria [Mrs. Mary—for that was her name], it is a great pleasure for us to have your daughter and your son and you with us in this church. I would also be very grateful to God if your husband would join us."

"My husband is a very dangerous man, *Senhor*," the woman replied, and somehow, I believed her.

"Please invite him to be my guest tomorrow night, *Senhora*," I said, and I wondered just what kind of man he could be to merit such fear and respect in that country of dangerous men.

On the final evening of our inauguration services the church was almost full when little Maria came with her brother, her mother, and a big, brown man with a hard face and penetrating eyes. The family had to sit almost in the front row, so I was very much aware of the man they

86

had described as "very dangerous" as he watched those of us on the front platform.

When I gave the invitation that night, many people made their way forward to confess Christ and begin the necessary study for church membership. Among them was Maria's father. His family stood with him at the front of the church and they were the last we came to for special prayer and instruction. When I got to Maria's family I reached out to shake the hand of the big man.

"I am glad you have come," I said. "Your name, *Senhor?*"

"Call me Jose," he answered in a deep, husky voice. And I thought, I'll be glad to call you any name you choose.

"Would you like to become a Christian, *Senhor* Jose?" I asked.

"I need to talk with you in private first," the big man answered, and I did not like that idea at all. The only private place we had was the Sunday school room behind the sanctuary, and it was dark back there. Dangerous men in that country were usually very fast and final with a gun or knife at close range and I was reluctant to be alone with this man. But after all, I had invited him to come as my special guest, and he had come forward and wanted to talk with me. I figured I owed him a hearing, so we moved to the back room where he talked to me in the flickering candlelight.

"Before you can let me be a Christian in this church, there are some things you must know about me, *Senhor*," he said. "I know what it means to be a Christian. I want my family to grow up in God's church and to study and follow the teachings of the Bible. I have always wanted to do what is right, and God knows I have tried. But I got pushed too far in Mato Grosso state and had to kill a man. It would have been all right, *Senhor*, because that man was a killer by nature and he forced the fight. I had to do it to save my family, and I would do it again, if necessary. The good people in the village there are grateful. But his brother is the local sheriff and two other brothers enjoy killing people also. If I had stayed, I would have had to kill the three brothers. That would have left two widows with children, and it would have put me outside the law. So I ran away with my family to avoid more killing. I am afraid of no man, *Senhor*, especially not of the cowardly killers back there in Mato Grosso who hide behind a badge to do their killing.

"Now I have two questions for you *Senhor*. First, do you think God will have me? And second, do you still want me in this church?"

My answer to the big Indian was "Yes, to both questions." He broke down and cried when he talked with God, confessed his sins, and asked God to forgive him. And I prayed for God to help Jose be a good Christian husband and father, and to control his violent nature when people pushed him too hard.

"You are greatly blessed, *Senhor* Jose," I said as we made our way back to his waiting family. "You have a good wife, a fine son, and little Maria, who has brought her whole family to Christ and to his church."

As the years rolled by and my mission field moved to new areas of the country, pastoral care for the people of New Glory passed to Brazilian leadership. I gradually lost track of Jose's family. He and his wife and son disappeared from the area and none of the New Glory Christians could tell me where they had gone. (People with a violent past like Jose's usually have to keep moving to avoid finishing what was started before they became Christians.) But little Maria grew to become a beautiful young lady. She felt called by God to mission service and Merry and I were able to help her study in preparation for that work. After her graduation from Mission Training School, she married a young man who shared her calling and moved into new country west of Mato Grosso for mission service.

"Let the little children come to me, and do not hinder them, for the kingdom of God belongs to such as these" (Mark 10:14–16).

88

14

Dona Edite of Porangatu

The angel said to the women, "Do not be afraid, for I know that you are looking for Jesus, who was crucified. He is not here; he has risen, just as he said. Come and see the place where he lay. Then go quickly and tell his disciples: 'He has risen from the dead and is going ahead of you into Galilee. There you will see him.' Now I have told you."

So the women hurried away from the tomb, afraid yet filled with joy, and ran to tell his disciples. Suddenly Jesus met them. "Greetings," he said. They came to him, clasped his feet and worshiped him. Then Jesus said to them, "Do not be afraid. Go and tell my brothers to go to Galilee; there they will see me" (Matt. 28:5-10).

The large, brown woman seemed nervous. She kept looking toward the outer circle of people standing in the darkness.

"Are you expecting someone?" I asked her.

"She is afraid of her husband," one of the other women said, "and she has reason to be afraid."

Edite—for that was her name—soon faded into the

darkness. She had been among the several women who had just become Christians following a street meeting on the poor side of Porangatu, Brazil. I asked the others if they knew her.

"Yes, we all know Edite," said one of the women. "Her six wild boys are the terror of the town."

"They're the main ones who broke all the windows out of our new school building last week," said another of the women.

"And the police are questioning them about other crimes as well," added another.

I asked them about Edite's husband.

"Her husband comes and goes."

"He is a mean, difficult man."

"You don't want to have anything to do with him, Pastor."

"He's all bad news around here."

I learned that her husband's name was Raimundo. I asked what kind of work he did.

"He fishes most of the time."

"Sometimes he works on cars."

"And sometimes he just goes off into the brush for a month or so."

About one month after our street meeting the new chapel was finished and inauguration services filled the sanctuary. At the invitation concluding the service, Edite came forward and stood before me. Two little boys held on to her dress, she held a large baby in her arms, and she was near to giving birth to another. Tears streamed down her face as she spoke to me.

"Pastor, can a woman who can neither read nor write be a member of this church?"

"Yes, *Dona* [Madam], you can be a member here but you will have to work hard to be the kind of Christian this church needs."

Her face brightened. "Hard work is all I know," she said. "Tell me what to do and I will work hard for the Lord."

90

Along with all the others who had come forward, Edite was assigned a Bible verse to be memorized and repeated to me before the service next evening. When she came early to say her Bible verse, there was a new woman with her. After the service the two of them came forward.

"Pastor, this is my neighbor," said Edite. "She helped me memorize my Bible verse for today. I am so dumb and she worked so hard teaching me, she wants to become a Christian also."

On the third night of services Edite came forward with another woman: "This is my neighbor who washes clothes with me at the creek. She helped me memorize my verse for today, and she too wants to become a Christian."

The final night Edite came with a third woman who had also helped her memorize and who also wanted to become a Christian. New Christians were given twenty-three verses to memorize along with the regular teaching we offered people to prepare them for membership in the new church. During her first month as a Christian, Edite won five people to Christ, always using the same humble approach, "I am so .dumb. Will you help me?"

Raimundo was enraged with his wife for wanting to become a Christian. Furthermore, he did not want her to learn anything; Edite's job was to work hard and to have babies.

I offered to go talk with Raimundo, but was warned to stay away. "He swears he will kill you, Pastor, because you have made a Christian out of his wife," someone told me.

Raimundo beat his wife and threatened to kill her, and when the neighbor women threatened to go to the police, he abandoned his family, saying, "If you want to be a Christian, then let the Christians take care of you."

Edite was left with six children and a baby due any day. She had no income other than from the laundry she took in; she washed it in the creek and ironed it with a charcoal iron. The Christians helped to feed the family and the good women took over when the baby was born. Her boys did not have time to get into much trouble during those difficult days—each was busy delivering clothes or doing odd jobs around town.

Other changes began taking place in the boys as well. When I bought a new soccer football and volleyball for the young people of the church, I announced, "This new church is God's house in this community. It has new, beautiful windows. If any of these windows are broken by bad boys throwing rocks, I will collect the balls and there will be no more playing on the church property."

Only one rock was thrown at the new church—and one frightened boy was educated by Edite's sons never to throw rocks again. No rowdy community was ever policed so thoroughly as Porangatu West during those days. I never asked about "police brutality" and no young person ever mentioned having to be talked to twice by Edite's big boys. One after another the boys became Christians, memorized their Bible verses, and became members of Sunday school and church.

For six months nothing was heard of Raimundo. It seemed that he had indeed gone away for good. Then one day a truck pulled up in front of Edite's house and a very sick man was pulled out and left at the door. Raimundo seemed to be dying. Edite sent one of her boys for Merry and me, and we came at once. Malaria had been with us for years, so diagnosing the problem took much less time than curing it.

"What are you going to do?" asked Raimundo weakly when I rolled him over.

"You wanted to stab me, Raimundo. Now I am going to stab you," I said as I gave him a shot. "You wanted to kill me. Now we are going to give you back your life. You left your family for the Christians to take care of, and now the Christians are taking care of you. When you are better you will owe me two things, and I intend to collect."

With rest and treatment Raimundo recovered quickly from his dangerous case of malaria. He began appearing in church as soon as he could move around. After about two months he came to see me.

"You said I owe you two things and that you intend to collect," he said. "What do I owe you, Pastor?"

"First, Raimundo, you know where there is an excellent place to catch large-mouthed bass near here. I want you to take me fishing there." (That fishing place of his was a well-kept secret.)

"We will go when you are ready," he said. "What else do I owe?"

"You owe your life to God and to God's people who have taken care of your family while you were gone—and who have taken care of you since you came back. Now I want you to confess your sins and surrender your life to Jesus Christ."

"I have wanted to do that for a long time, Pastor, but I have been ashamed."

When it was time for Edite to make her profession of faith I invited her to stand before the congregation to give her testimony and to repeat the Bible verses she had learned. She repeated all twenty-three of them perfectly and with feeling, then turned to the Book of Romans and began reading with skill and clarity:

> I urge you brothers, in view of God's mercy, to offer your bodies as living sacrifices, holy and pleasing to God—which is your spiritual worship. Do not conform any longer to the pattern of this world, but be transformed by the renewing of your mind (Rom. 12:1-2).

She continued to read from the same chapter concerning the spiritual gifts God gives to all his servants, enabling them to serve him well.

> Never be lacking in zeal, but keep your spiritual fervor, serving the Lord. Be joyful in hope, patient in affliction, faithful in prayer. Share with God's people who are in need. Practice hospitality (vv. 11-13).

Edite's face shone like an angel as she stood before a congregation that had suffered with her through hard times.

"Edite, you have learned to read," I said with delight. "Who taught you?" (I already knew about the nightly meetings for all the new Christians who couldn't read.) Edite pointed to a small black woman who had been reared in an Indian village by a missionary lady.

"Lydia taught us all to read and write, and we thank God for her," Edite said, tears of joy in her eyes.

Raimundo kept his word and became a good member of the church and of the community. He was a very good automobile mechanic and, with tools that I lent him, he set up a shop and supported his family well. Both he and his wife continued to quietly witness to others concerning the good things God had brought into their lives.

Several years after my departure from north Goias, I returned to the town of Ceres for a special meeting. I was delighted to see *Dona* Edite and *Senhor* Raimundo sitting happily in the congregation. After the service I greeted them.

"It is good to see both of you again. What are you doing in Ceres now, and why did you leave Porangatu?"

"The boys are ready for college now," Raimundo said with quiet pride. "We moved so they could go on with their education."

"Our oldest boy is in law school now," said Edite. "And the second boy wants to be a doctor. He is in university now and is doing well. It takes time when we all have to work to pay the bills."

Law school and medicine, I thought. How far my village vigilantes had come in such a short time. "What about the others?" I asked, "and how many children do you have now?"

"God has given us only eight," Edite said a little sadly, "but we are grateful for all he has given."

"And do you both still look for non-Christian neighbors to talk with about Christ?" I asked.

"Yes, Pastor," they replied. "How can we keep silent when God has done so much for us?"

I recall a question I once asked a group of women in Porangatu: "Why do you think Jesus sent women to be his first missionaries?" And I remember Edite's answer: "Because they loved him the most."

Through the years of mission service I have noticed that when God has a difficult and dangerous job to be done, he frequently sends Christian women. Violent men tend to respond to opposition with violence, but women like Edite know how to witness, suffer, be humble, and keep on witnessing. It is a gift of God's Spirit which she continues to use for his glory.

"Do not be afraid," Jesus said, "Go and tell. . . ."

15

Benigno and the World of Spirits

After Jesus had gone indoors, his disciples asked him privately, "Why couldn't we drive [the spirit] out?"

He replied, "This kind can come out only by prayer (Mark 9:28-29).[1]

The dark world of spirits remains an obscure one to most of us in modern society. Our scientific educational system normally rejects any possibility that spirit beings exist capable of interfering in the lives of humans. We North Americans are taught to treat the occult as childish superstition, and are therefore quite unprepared to help people under demonic influence. People like Senhor Benigno, for example.

I met *Senhor* Benigno and his wife Marta at a street meeting in the town of Gurupi in 1963 when the Brasilia–Belém highway was being constructed through north Goias State. The couple, looking angry and

---

1. Some manuscripts read "prayer and fasting" (NIV).

dangerous, laughed and yelled as they tried to distract the men and women who stood in the dusty street listening to Patricio Lili, a great Indian preacher.

After the street meeting I asked the evangelist why Benigno and Marta were so opposed to the gospel.

"They are both under the direction of evil spirits," Patricio explained. "Only God will be able to change their attitudes and their lives. They are slaves to spirits who oppose us."

"How do you know this, Patricio?"

"Because I live and work among Indian tribes where evil spirits have powerful influence. You come from worlds where the devil must use other methods to accomplish his purposes."

That gave me a lot to think about. I had come from Congo in 1962 to our new work in Brazil, so evil spirit activity was not new to me, nor did I underestimate its power.

Benigno, who was part Negro and part Brazilian Indian, had roots in both African and Indian spiritism and was a noted spirit medium in Gurupi and the surrounding area. His Brazilian Indian wife received her power to communicate with spirits through her Indian heritage. Both of them had started talking only with good spirits, they later explained, because they wanted to help people. Gradually they drifted into communication with more powerful spirits who offered them more power and, in return, demanded more complete obedience.

The next evening we moved our evangelistic meeting to a small shed near the place where we wanted to build a church. Some sixty people crowded inside to hear Patricio; an equal number were standing in the street, looking through the open windows and trying to hear. I was not pleased to find Benigno and his wife sitting near the front of the crowd.

"This could be a long evening, Patricio," I said, looking at the unwanted guests.

"Or it could be a very short one," Patricio observed with a smile.

Angry comments and objections from the two punctuated

the powerful preaching of Patricio. Some members of the audience tried to throw both Benigno and Marta out of the meeting, but I objected. "Leave them here," I said. "These people need to hear about God's love in Christ and his power to free men from the devil more than most of us here." And to the two objectors I said, "Please sit quietly and listen to what God has to say to you tonight. If you don't like what you hear, then go away. But don't try to break up this meeting. You will find yourself fighting against God and you will lose."

Angry eyes watched Patricio and me throughout the remainder of the service. When it was over, I asked the couple if they would like us to have a special prayer for them. "I can see there are battles going on in both of you," I explained.

Marta swore at me and pushed her way through the crowd. Benigno, probably more to oppose his wife than a desire for prayer, answered, "Yes, I would like a prayer."

Marta shouted from the door, "You are crazy, Benigno!" (I did not understand what he replied to her.) Then Benigno, Patricio, and I bowed in prayer, asking God to free this man who was bound by Satan. Although he remained silent, when he looked at me after that prayer his eyes revealed a man who had seen hell and now had hope. However, Benigno's was no sudden conversion. When he reached the street he went directly to his wife, knocked her to the ground, and began pounding her with all his force. Suddenly she threw him off and leaped to her feet, and the two of them stood swinging hard blows and curses at each other.

"Nice family, that one," I commented as they moved on down the street.

"They've been at it for a long time, Pastor. It's a wonder that they don't kill each other. They are both well-known spirit mediums here, and each is jealous of the other's power and influence.

B enigno owned a primitive brick kiln near town.

99

We contracted to buy bricks from him for the construction of the church and manse. He seemed surprised that we would deal with him, but his bricks were the best available, his price was the lowest around, and his ox carts delivered on schedule.

On each visit to Gurupi I looked forward to quiet visits with Benigno and opportunities to respond to his questions about Christianity. Gradually the hate inside him was replaced by a longing to know more about God's gospel. He became a regular front-row member at our meetings and joined a Sunday school class for people wanting to know more about Christianity.

Before six months were up, Benigno had become a Christian. But he was still far from free of the evil spirits that oppressed him. His exit from the spirit world was not unlike a person overcoming alcohol or drug addiction. Supported by a spiritual brother, Ricardo, who had escaped from spiritism and was now a strong Christian, Benigno struggled for six months against spiritual oppression and despair before finally being freed by prayer and fasting.

"What made you become a Christian?" I asked Benigno one day.

"My brick business can only function during the dry season, Pastor, so I needed an extra job to feed my family. I traveled during the rains as a peddler and made good money. But every time I came back with money for more goods, I was robbed by a man with a gun. I had only a knife for defense, and I am good with a knife, but I could not reach him with his gun. Every time I came back, he would hide and make me lay down my money and goods and walk away. I was furious. This lazy man did no work, but took my money and property. I talked with my spirits about this problem and tried to put a curse on the robber. It didn't work. Finally, one of my spirits told me to go to the 'Queen of the Araguaia,' and he told me where I could find her."

Benigno told me how he walked three days in the forest to the place his spirits said the "Queen" would be found. When he came into the clearing and hailed the house, a voice answered, "Come in Benigno. I have been expecting you."

He entered the grass-roofed hut and saw an old woman sitting behind a table. "How did you know my name?" he asked her.

"I have seen you since you left your home in Gurupi and I have watched you cross the forest," the woman replied. "You have come for power to curse your enemy, and you are a fool."

"Why do you call me a fool?"

"Look at that wall," she said, pointing to a picture. "What do you see?"

"I see a deer running from dogs, and a hunter waiting for the deer to come close to him."

"God gives dumb creatures sense enough to run from danger, Benigno. Yet you, a man, are a fool. You want to fight with your knife a man who has a gun. You should run away and save your life. Stop being a fool. What do you see on the other wall?"

"I see books—many books."

"They are the books of my trade. They tell me much of the unseen world and how to enter it and find power to oppose enemies. But the spirits' price is slavery, Benigno. Now what do you see on the table?"

"I see a book."

"What kind of book?" It was a Bible.

"What you need, Benigno, is not spirit power to kill your enemy, but God's power to give you life. Go, buy yourself a Bible. Read it, and follow its teachings. Don't be a fool any longer."

"I bought a Bible and began reading it when I got back home," Benigno said, "and then I began talking with you Christians who helped explain to me how to become a Christian."

When Marta saw that her husband had escaped spirit oppression, she also turned to Christ and began the long, slow process of "coming out." Later, when people wanted to become Christians and escape from spirit bondage, we

101

assigned Benigno as an "older spiritual brother" or Marta as an "older spiritual sister" to the individuals, to pray and fast with them on their way to freedom. Only those who have come out know the intensity of the struggle. Long ago Jesus said, "This kind [of spirit] can come out only by prayer."

When the heavy rains begin to fall in north Goias, and waters rise over the brick kiln of *Senhor* Benigno, this quiet Christian saddles his riding mule, loads his pack mules with Bibles, Christian literature, and necessary supplies, and moves out into the big, lonely country. He travels slowly from homestead to homestead, visiting people, sharing God's gospel, and praying for God's power in their lives. For three months of each year Benigno becomes God's peddler. No longer a fool, now he is guided by the teachings of the Bible. He knows what it is to be enslaved by evil spirits, and he knows that the only way to freedom is through the power of prayer in God's Holy Spirit.

16

Javaé

Jesus went through all the towns and villages, teaching in their synagogues, preaching the good news of the kingdom. . . . When he saw the crowds, he had compassion on them, because they were harassed and helpless, like sheep without a shepherd. Then he said to his disciples, "The harvest is plentiful but the workers are few. Ask the Lord of the harvest, therefore, to send out workers into his harvest field" (Matt. 9:35-38).

Patricio and I climbed toward cruise altitude as the morning sun climbed over the Brazilian jungle toward the eastern horizon. We were on our way home after an extended evangelistic journey, and were looking forward to a bath, good food, and rest, when I saw a thin wisp of smoke rising from a small clearing in the forest. As we circled for a closer look, women, children, and dogs from a small Indian village ran into the forest, but one large Indian stood in the clearing and shook his fist at us.

"That, Patricio, is the Javaé," I said, referring to a group of unevangelized and uncivilized Indians living near the

Araguaia River. "They don't like strangers in their lands or airplanes scaring their women and children."

"My civilized brother," said my friend, "those Javaé down there are my people. They are born in these forests, they live their whole lives in the forest, and they die in the forest darkness having never heard the name of Jesus Christ. They know nothing of God's love for them revealed to us in Christ.

"You are doing so much for the civilized in this field," he continued, tears rolling down his brown cheeks. "All along the new highways you have evangelistic services, you build churches, open schools, help provide medical aid. When are you going to do something to help the Javaé know and follow Christ?"

Some questions are not easy to answer. I thought about that one a long time before responding, "When God opens the door, I will go in to them." During the long silence of our flight across the forests of the Javaé, I thought about Jesus and his concern for unreached people, and I felt like God had spoken to me through Patricio.

Several months later, I was again flying over the forests of the Javaé, this time with my son, Paul, Jr., and Jim Lumheim, a veteran mission pilot. Near the border of the reservation I noticed several long dugout canoes and a fishing camp. There was a government trading post nearby with a short landing strip. Although the Javaé live secluded in a forest preserve along the banks of the Araguaia River, and though they do not welcome invaders or the uninvited and are unimpressed with the benefits of civilization, they do come out of their forests from time to time in order to trade.

"It looks like God has opened the door to the Javaé," I said to my colleagues, "so let's give it a try. They must be friendly now since they have come out to trade."

When the plane engine was shut down we were surrounded by an excited group of children. They seemed friendly, especially when I gave them a few balls to play

104

with. We made our way to the camp with excited little Indians crowding around us. The first adult we encountered was a large man wearing Levi pants. Levis were hard to come by in that country so I assumed this man could speak Portuguese.

"*Bom dia, Amigo* [Good day, friend]," I said, with a big smile.

As he returned my greeting using good Portuguese, the man did a very strange thing for an Indian: he smiled. "*Bom dia, Senhor*," he said.

I have been told that no self-respecting Indian will smile at a stranger unless he sees something you have that he intends to take from you, or unless he is a Christian who has learned to trust non-Indians. So I asked the man in Levis, "Are you a Christian?"

"Yes, I am a Christian," he replied.

I was amazed, because I had been told that no mission work had been done among the Javaé.

"Are there other Christians here?" I asked.

"Yes, we are all Christians here."

All those naked people running around did not look like Christians to me, but I am not sure what naked Christians are supposed to look like. I wanted to prolong the conversation, so I removed my straw hat, wiped my head, and said, "It is hot in the sun, is it not, *Amigo*?"

"It is hot, *Senhor*. Will you sit in my shade?" He indicated a grass-covered shelter nearby. We entered (my colleagues had moved on to talk with others) and he sat on a log. I looked around for a place to sit and selected a pile of dry grass. When I sat down on the hay, I noticed a strange expression flit across the face of my host. A small baby was sitting on the sand between us, and its loud crying made conversation with my new friend very difficult.

"Is that your baby?" I asked, hoping a mother would show up to take him away.

"That is my son."

"Does your son have a mother?"

"Yes."

"Is she near?" I asked, with rising hope for a better conversation.

"You are sitting on her," the Indian said.

Sure enough, when I looked at the pile of hay, I saw two feet sticking out of one end. I stood up and stepped forward and the grass bed exploded behind me. A very naked and very angry Indian woman pushed past me and ran outside yelling things I did not understand nor care to. My host rolled off his log laughing louder than Christian courtesy should permit. The woman stopped about twenty paces from the shelter, turned around, and came running back toward me at high speed. I didn't like the looks of things at that point, so I stepped behind the center pole, hoping it would slow her down somewhat. She grabbed that crying baby and headed out again, still yelling and still very angry. The shelter filled with laughing Indians. It was too late for very much quiet Christian conversation, so I moved on to the trading post.

"Are all these Indians Christians?" I asked the storekeeper.

"By their standards, they are," the man replied.

"What do you mean, 'by their standards'?"

"By their standards, they're Christians when they're not killing white people, and they are all being Christians right now." (It is against Brazilian law to kill an Indian, but not against Indian law to kill a non-Indian.)

"But I thought no mission work had been done among the Javaé," I answered.

"These are not Javaé. They are Caraja and they have had missionaries working with them for years."

Back in the airplane I prayed, "Lord, I tried. But there has got to be a better way to evangelize Indians than by sitting on their women."

A year or so after my attempt to enter an open door to the Javaé, I was again flying over their lands. On the border of the reservation I saw a canoe moving toward

106

a fishing camp. There was a large ranch across the river and an airstrip. I landed and asked the Indian cowboy who rode up to my plane, "Are those Indians over there Javaé?"

"Yes," he answered.

I cranked up the engine and flew away. I wondered what that cowboy thought when I flew away with so little information, but it was all I needed. God had again opened a door, and this time I intended to use it correctly. When I arrived at my home town in Porangatu, I sent a telegram to Patricio saying: "The door to the Javaé is open. Come and we will enter together."

Two weeks later Patricio arrived and we flew the next day to the ranch, where we borrowed a canoe. Crossing the river, we approached what turned out to be much more than just a fishing camp; it was more of a permanent village. For a moment my missionary dreams began to take beautiful form. But as we paddled closer to the village, I didn't like what I saw. There were no women or children in sight. No one waited at the landing. And up on a higher bank stood a line of very big, well-armed Indian warriors, silent and obviously unfriendly. This was not the warm welcome I had hoped for, and I was glad that Patricio— with his shirt open and his long, black hair blowing in the breeze—was sitting in the bow of the canoe: we needed all the Indian identity we could get right then.

When I beached the canoe, Patricio stepped out like a commanding general. He walked with confidence toward the waiting warriors and did not hesitate when the line of men began advancing toward us. I thought about just letting Patricio talk with them, but knowing I'd have to live with myself afterward, I too walked up to meet the advancing warriors. We were surrounded and escorted to the council ring of the village. The Javaé were talking to Patricio and seemed rather angry, but I couldn't understand a word they said.

"Why are the men angry?" I asked a nice-looking Indian standing near me. He was wearing Brazilian paratrooper boots so I assumed he could speak Portuguese.

"They are unhappy you kept us waiting," he answered,

107

and I wondered how we could have kept them waiting when they didn't even know we were coming.

On our way to the council ring, we were confronted by a small, rather young Brazilian who shouted, "Stop. I forbid you to enter my village!"

"Who are you?" Patricio answered, moving close to the threatening little man.

"I am the representative of FUNAI[1] for this region. I will not permit you to enter."

"Who are you to order me off Indian land?" my evangelist friend answered with a rising anger I had never seen before. "I am a native Brazilian Indian, and no non-Indian orders me off of any Indian land. By the laws of your people, any Indian goes where he pleases on Indian lands. Stand aside, young man." And Patricio walked straight at the agent, who wisely moved out of his path.

"You bit the big one, boy," I said, walking up to the angry, somewhat frightened man.

"Who is he?"

"That is Patricio Lili. Haven't you heard of him? He has placed his nephews in high places in politics in Mato Grosso. One is mayor of a large city. Another is a senator. And Patricio has direct access to the president in Brasilia. You better leave him alone."

"Then *you* can't come in," he said rudely.

"I fly with the big boy. Are you sure you want to try to stop me?" I said, not liking his attitude. "And I fly anywhere in Brazil with authorization of the commanding general of the Air Force," I added, and with that I walked on past, wondering as I did what problems we would have from him.[2]

In the shade at the council circle Patricio and I sat with the men of the Javaé. The warriors were laughing and in a good mood after Patricio's encounter with the agent, so

1. FUNAI, the Brazilian department for the preservation and protection of the Indians, claimed sole jurisdiction over them; no mission work was permitted.

2. I would later save the agent's life by flying him out for treatment after he was bitten by a rabid dog. He returned the favor by denouncing our mission work to the authorities. Sometimes it hurts to help people.

I gathered that FUNAI's representative was not very popular in this village. Patricio was invited to tell why we had come to the Javaé. Because he was using a language I didn't understand, I had no idea what he was saying but I was confident God was giving him the right words. When he finished his short address, the men began commenting in turn, apparently expressing their reactions to what had been said. Each of the men kept his remarks to no more than five minutes, but with about twenty men making comments, it took time to work around the circle. When they had finished, the leader turned to me and said, "Now you speak."

I was not very deep in Brazilian Indian culture at that time, since most of my work had been with non-Indians in frontier areas, so I leaned on my African experiences and trusted God to give me the right words to say to tribal people. I spoke in Portuguese and the Indian with the paratrooper boots translated into Javaé. In brief, my message followed tribal thinking in a tribal world view:

"The Creator God made all things—the Araguaia River and all great rivers with their abundance of fish for food, the forests and all the animals and birds in them. He made all men and placed each people in their sacred hunting grounds. He made the Javaé and has given you a good land with much wild game and many fish. It is a good place to live and to raise your children. But the Creator God is angry.

"Why is the Creator God angry? Because he loves his tribesmen whom he has made, but his tribesmen no longer worship him nor try to follow his ways. He sent his Son to call the tribes back to those ways, but the warriors hung the Son on a tree and killed him. They left his dead body for all to see, but God gave his Son new life and called him back to his village in the sky. But God is still lonely for his people who do not know him, love him, or follow his ways. That is why the Creator God has sent my brother, Patricio, and me to visit the Javaé and to give you God's message. We have come to point you to the path which will lead you back to his ways."

I sat down and prayed silently, "Lord, please fill in the gaps and enable them to understand."

As the men had done with the message of Patricio, each commented on what I had said until the entire circle of men had spoken. Then we followed a wonderful Indian custom—we all stretched out in the shade and went to sleep. Before I had fallen asleep, Patricio asked me if I had told anyone that we were coming there.

"No," I answered him. "Why?"

"Because they knew we were coming. That's why they seemed angry when we came. The leading men of all the Javaé villages from all over the reservation have been waiting here for five days to hear a message of great importance which was to be brought to them by an Indian from far away."

"But how did they get such a message?" I asked.

"The Javaé told them," Patricio answered. Then he stretched out on a log and went to sleep.

I wondered, as I too drifted off, whether I would ever understand the mysteries of the Javaé.

(We found out later that the FUNAI representative had asked why leaders were gathering from all over the reservation. When he was told that an Indian was arriving with a message of great importance for them, he warned them not to receive the "troublemaker," but to run him out of the village. He got the men together and ready for battle, and was probably quite upset when they gave us the opportunity to speak. Indians have a way of doing what they want to do, especially on their own turf.)

At the ranch headquarters across the river we had accepted the invitation of the director, Dr. Nelson, to have a meeting that night for his cowboys and other ranch hands. I agreed to do so because I had wanted to make sure we would be missed if we didn't come back from our visit to the village. After sitting with the Javaé all afternoon, Patricio and I invited them to come with us and take part

110

in the service. Several of the Indian men were working at the ranch as cowboys, and relationships were cordial between the Javaé and the ranch personnel.

Our meeting in the moonlit yard of the ranch headquarters was a very memorable occasion. Indians and non-Indians sat together with trust and good will. And a friendship was established with Dr. Nelson which had a far-reaching influence on our work with the Javaé. Patricio's music and preaching made a profound impression on the rancher and he offered to build a school for Indians and ranch children if I would promise to direct it and to supply Christian teachers. (In due time a beautiful school was built and our mission was able to supply a Christian director and some excellent teachers.)

Because the time Patricio could give to the Javaé was limited, we left them with the promise to return as soon as we could. I was able to return once a month with outstanding Brazilian workers whose music and warm, Christian witness continued to build on our good beginning. On each trip I brought meat, medicine, and magazines to the FUNAI worker, attempting to overcome our disagreeable beginning.

To work effectively with Indians (or anyone else, for that matter) one must learn their language and spend significant time with them. Lasting work with Indians demands that one must love them, and love like that is a gift of God. I prayed for God's direction with a sincere desire to work with the Javaé. The Lord, however, gave me no liberty to leave the field of ten congregations I was then serving in north Goias. He did lead me, however, to a wonderful missionary family of the New Tribes Mission who had completed their work among the Caraja, cousins of the Javaé. Edward and Marguerite Harper were looking for a new work and, responding to God's direction, began serving the Javaé. I helped by providing air transportation, meat, and mail service, and our home served as a place for rest and recuperation. The Harpers lived with the Indians, worked with them, suffered with them; they learned their language and began translating Scripture for the Javaé people. Our

111

school across the river began growing. The future looked bright.

Once a month I sat with the Javaé. I sat with the arrow maker and admired his skill and artistry. Using stone tips secured with forest glue and wrappings, and using colorful parrot feathers to balance and direct the flight, the old man's arrows were works of art. Each arrow was also marked with strange markings of the tribe.

"And what do these markings mean?" I asked.

"Javaé," was the only answer.

I also sat with the old man whose specialty was carving canoe paddles. He too produced beautiful works of art, and finished his work with the markings of the tribe.

"What do these markings mean?" I asked.

"Javaé," he answered.

One morning before I flew out of the village, the old paddle carver presented me with a beautiful paddle. "This is for you to keep and use," he said.

"It is beautiful, Sir, and I will keep it always. Do you make paddles to sell?"

"Yes, I make paddles to sell, but this one is not for sale. It is Javaé."

"On my next trip, I will buy three paddles from you, if you would like to sell them to me," I said. But when my order was filled, they were very inferior and had no markings. "Why the difference in quality?" I asked my friend.

"These are not Javaé. They are for sale."

During one of my visits to the tribe, a three-day party was taking place. Games and contests included all the members of the village. I saw the men lining up for an archery contest, so I got in the line with the men and boys. (I hunted squirrels with bow and arrows as a boy in West Virginia, so why not try shooting with the men? Of course, I had never killed a squirrel with an arrow, but I had made them run.) When I took my place at the end

112

of the line of men, they all laughed and pushed me toward the line of women.

"You will have to win there before you can shoot with men," they yelled, laughing.

I borrowed arrows and a fine-looking bow from one of the women and, standing at the end of the line, took my turn. I beat them all. Those good arrows flew true and firm into the bull's eye of the target, and all three arrows were closely grouped. I was pleased and surprised, and the men all shouted and welcomed me into their line. But the women were not ready to let me go. They grabbed and held me and called a small, skinny woman to shoot. She put every arrow in the very center of the bull's eye, much better than anything I could do. The women all laughed and I sat with the old men to watch the finals. It was fun to be included in their games even though I was not up to the competition.

A while later two very big men with more muscles than a man should be allowed to have came to invite me to wrestle with the men. One look at those two made me very sure I wanted no part of that one. So I replied, "You would make me wrestle with your women first. I will sit with the fathers." They laughed and went away, and when I saw their battles, I was glad for the choice I had made.

About noon, when the sun was very hot, a group of women caught a large group of the men with a large, hemp hoop. With much yelling and good humor the women pulled the big men over the river bank and into the river. The men fought and yelled on the way, grabbing as many women as they could to fall with them into the river. That seemed to be the signal for resting time.

At intervals of about one hour throughout the day and night two warriors came from the spirit house, dressed in grass skirts, awesome head masks, and colorfully painted legs and bodies. With special music from native horns, whistles, and drums, the men performed a ritual dance with perfect rhythm and in perfect patterns.

"What does all this mean?" I asked, sitting next to my two Indian artisan friends.

113

"Javaé," was the anticipated answer.

"When will I understand the Javaé?" I asked, not expecting an answer. The reply surprised me.

"When you sit with the Javaé, you will understand. Come sit with us in the spirit house."

At the door of the house, I hesitated. In Africa, for a foreigner to enter the spirit house meant certain, sudden death. I was not at all sure I wanted to find out any more about the Javaé. But the two old men had already entered the hut, and were watching me. I entered, looked around, and sat on a log between my artisan friends. Smoke was rising from a small fire. The oldest man in the village was heating containers of colorful paint and helping two very powerful warriors paint themselves for the next ritual dance. When the two dancers were thoroughly Javaé, they donned their grass skirts and head dresses, and moved out into the clearing to perform their dance. I sat in silence with the old men in the house where the spirits of the Javaé lived. Great peace and quietness rested on the faces of these men, and strangely, I did not feel the presence of evil among us as I had in African spirit worship. At length, one of the men spoke.

"It is good to sit with the Javaé, is it not, my friend?"

"Yes, it is good," I answered.

We had a wonderful meeting on the moonlit riverbank that night. I was invited to tell more about the Creator God and how the Javaé could get back into communication with him and please him. I asked my friend with the paratrooper boots to pray to the Creator God before I began talking.

"I don't want to pray now," he said, teaching me something more about Indians.

"Fine," I answered. "Perhaps sometime you will want to talk with him." (I believe in letting big Indians do what they want to do, especially in their village.)

About halfway through my fifteen-minute talk, my booted friend stood up and said, "I pray now." And he prayed. I had no idea what he said (in Javaé) but Ed Harper

114

told me later that it was a good prayer. Then everyone discussed what I had been saying.

After the service a dark, powerfully built Indian said to me, "Tomorrow I will take you to the place of the big bass. There you will catch him." It took only one glance at this unfriendly looking individual to convince me not to be caught alone with him in the forest, so I answered him, "You are good to be willing to take me to the 'big one,' but let him grow bigger. I will take him later." The big man seemed angry with my answer, so I felt sure I had made a good decision.

"You were wise not to go with him," my booted friend soon informed me. "He wants your belt buckle and your fishing rod. You would not have returned. Tomorrow I will show you a big bass, if you want me to."

"Do you want my belt buckle or my fishing rod?" I answered, laughing. At daylight I stood with him on the riverbank ready to catch the "big one."

"Wade in the water to midstream, then cast by the bank near the big tree," he said.

"Me, wade in water filled with piranha?" I said. "I don't care that much about fishing." (The rivers in that area were filled with the flesh-eating fish.)

"Piranha will not eat you now," he replied.

"Why not? They always like meat."

"The Javaé have told them not to eat you now," he explained with quiet confidence.

"Not to eat Javaé, or not to eat anybody?" I asked with obvious doubt.

"Come with me," he said and waded to midstream. I followed and within a few minutes caught a half dozen piranhas and three good-sized bass. (I found out later that there are certain times of the year the piranha are not dangerous. Perhaps the spirits of the Javaé told them not to eat us.)

The courageous Harper family suffered greatly during their eleven months with the Javaé. They knew

115

how to work with Indians and were willing to pay the high cost of sacrificial service, but just as the Javaé were beginning to understand, the storm broke. The missionaries were falsely accused of wrongdoing by outsiders and denounced to the authorities. Ed Harper was arrested by an army officer, beaten, and ejected from the tribe even though his presence and work was authorized by the Indian Department. Dr. Nelson forcefully intervened to prevent further abrogation of the law, but our work among the Javaé was finished. The Harpers moved to another tribe and continued their ministries. Merry and I moved to the Amazon Highway to begin new work, and the Javaé were left without the gospel and without help.

After talking with Patricio, Dr. Nelson offered two hundred acres of good grasslands outside the reservation to the Javaé and agreed to give them two hundred head of breeding stock to get started ranching. Patricio had told him the story of his people and their need to own land or property in order to become Brazilian citizens with rights beyond the reservation. Freedom from FUNAI is a common Indian dream, but authorities in Brasilia rejected Dr. Nelson's offer and cut off our efforts to help some of the Javaé become land-owning citizens.

(Dr. Nelson's friendship with the Javaé Indians did not extend to the *Cara Pretas* [Black Faces] who lived in the swamp at the end of his airstrip. These black Indians were descendants of African slaves who had escaped into the jungles and settled near the Javaé. Nelson ordered his cowboys to kill on sight any *Cara Pretas*, who usually killed cowboys and cows before they themselves were seen. I never enjoyed fishing in the areas of the *Cara Pretas*. They might see something I had they wanted.)

About six years after our departure from the Javaé, Ed Harper visited the tribe. Even though we had left no Christians among them, Ed found eighty adults professing faith in Christ and trying to follow his teachings. Among them was my friend with the boots, who had

116

become the chieftain of the Javaé and the leading Christian as well. Most of the Javaé children attended the Christian school at the ranch, and the Javaé Christians had even won some of the *Cara Pretas* to Christ and were helping them learn Christian ways. The Javaé were delighted to see Ed again and begged him to return to their village. They asked about his wife and family, and about the "Bird Man," as they called me.

"We miss him," they told him. "We want him to come back to fly in our skies."

Jesus is still concerned about people who run around like sheep without a shepherd—people helpless to do anything about their lost condition. He still commands his followers to share his concern for people who have not heard of God's gracious invitation to lost people. He still instructs his followers to pray to the Lord of the harvest to send out workers to save the crop before it is too late.

But praying for lost people and for sufficient workers to reach them can become costly: one can become involved, and becoming involved with unreached people may demand more than we really want to give. That is because God usually helps people in need through other people who care enough to become involved.

People cannot wait. Life moves on. Unreached people like the Javaé are born in the forest, live their whole lives in the forest, and die in the forest without ever hearing that God loves them, without ever hearing about salvation in Jesus Christ. It is always worth the cost to share Christ's compassion for the multitudes who live and die without him. And it is well worth the effort to sit with him among the Javaé. Because, as my old Indian friend told me, only when you sit with the Javaé will you understand.

17

The Faceless Fathers
of the Kuruaya

Now the Lord is the Spirit, and where the Spirit of the Lord is, there is freedom. And we, who with unveiled faces all reflect the Lord's glory, are being transformed into his likeness with ever-increasing glory, which comes from the Lord, who is the Spirit (2 Cor. 3:17-18).

In 1973 my wife and I moved to Altamira, Brazil, to begin a church-planting ministry along the new Trans-Amazon Highway. We built our home among Indian neighbors on the bank of the Xingu River. I was "patron" (boss) for those who worked on the construction of our home, and for the many little boys who worked and played in our yard. I was protector for some who needed help with the authorities. Merry and I provided transportation to the clinic and hospital for the sick, and my wife was twenty-four-hour neighborhood nurse. She consulted, prescribed, gave shots and advice, and often interceded for our friends with local medical authorities. I fished and hunted with the men, and swapped stories with them. We laughed, we sorrowed, we welcomed the new, we buried the dead. We were friends—and we loved them.

Scripture tells us that "unveiled faces" reflect the glory of God when his Spirit transforms his creatures into the likeness of their Creator. Veiled faces, however, still await the miracle, but in this life no one can wait for very long. People left behind the veil soon become faceless, like the "Faceless Fathers of the Kuruaya."

A tall Indian woman stands motionless at sunset on the bank of the Xingu River in the Amazon jungle of Brazil. Silent, deep in thought and worship, Payá keeps her nightly vigil. Payá lives her life on the bank of the Xingu, draws most of life's necessities from the river's richness, and seeks comfort from this, her nightly meditation at the water's edge. Uncharacteristically, she breaks her customary silence and speaks to me in a quiet, almost reverent voice.

"*Seu Paulo* [Mr. Paul], you love our river, don't you?"

"It is beautiful, neighbor, and at sunset it calms the soul," I answer.

After a brief silence, Payá continues. "It goes on and on. Nothing can stop it. It comes from where we do not know. It goes to where we have not been. It is like life, is it not, *Seu Paulo*?"

Yes, I think, the river *is* like life: it is always there, always moving; nothing can stop it. But the Xingu withholds its secrets even from the Kuruaya, and Payá does not have the answers to life's big problems. Now, after six years of living as next-door neighbors and friends, Payá for the first time asks me a religious question.

"*Seu Paulo*, do you know where our Xingu goes?"[1]

The Kuruayans I have known are not quick to talk with an outsider about their "Creator God," nor about their

1. Lucien Bodard, in his book *Green Hell*, says, "The Xingu is revered by the Indians as a sacred river; for them, it is the supreme lord of the universe, the master of water and fire. According to Indian myth, it was on the banks of the Xingu that the hero Maivutsini created the heavens, the earth and men; he made them all, good and bad alike. To the Indians, the good men are those they know, the men of their own tribe. The bad are the others, all the others." Lucien Bodard, *Green Hell, Massacre of the Brazilian Indians*. J. Monaghan, trans. (New York: Dutton, 1981).

120

ways of worship. Certainly they will not share their deep feelings with anyone whose sincerity and friendship they question. And Indians normally distrust everyone beyond their own tribe or larger family.

Although the Kuruaya now live among whites and other Indians along the Xingu River, they do not feel a part of the mixed society, nor do they wish to become a part of it. Numerous sociological problems accompany the conflicts in world views represented in the mixed community: there is no place in society for the warrior who fulfills the male image of the Kuruaya; the role of women has changed; and it remains very difficult for the tribesmen to identify the God of the Christians with the Creator God of the Kuruaya.

When we first met as neighbors, Payá had carefully explained the difference between her second husband (her first had been killed in a war) and herself. "My husband is *Cristao* [Christian]," she had said. "I am Kuruaya."

"Can't a Kuruaya be Christian?" I asked.

"Oh no. Kuruaya is Kuruaya. We follow the traditions of our people."

The picture of the Creator God of the Kuruaya came to me very slowly through daily contacts with the Kuruaya people. He is the one who made all nature and all people. He placed the Kuruaya in their holy ground on the banks of the Xingu. He is a good God who loves his people and hates the evil ones, who are sons of devils. (It is the sons of devils who have driven the Kuruaya from their holy lands where the spirits of the Kuruaya remain—without living tribesmen to honor them and consult with them for wisdom and direction.)

"The people of the Creator God are the Kuruaya," Payá quietly assures me.

"And the whites, like me?"

"Oh, you are other people. People of the Christian God," she replies.

Why is it so very difficult to convince the Kuruaya that the Christian God is the same as their Creator God? Why cannot a Kuruayan also be a Christian? I have two tentative answers to this question, both of which I would be happy to change. First, I believe the Kuruaya do not want to join the Christian tribe because they like their own tribe better. They haven't been convinced that the Christians are indeed brothers of the Kuruaya, nor do they feel that the Christian God can be their God and the God of their enemies as well. Another problem is, why has their Kuruayan God failed them?

The second reason for their reluctance to shift allegiance, or establish identity with the Christian God, is the fact that all the spirits of their larger family remain in the old world view. These spirits are reverenced, venerated, and at times consulted.

Nature, for the Kuruaya, is all part of the Creator God's activity, just as man is part of it all. Nature is good; plants and animals talk and admonish the tribesmen to do right; the great Xingu pulls it all together. The Kuruaya become different people when they leave the town to return to the forest and river.[2] In the forest they are relaxed and happy, and they talk with both animals and plants. Little-fat-pigeon, one of my good fishing friends, hooked a very large fish one day when we were together. He fought for about five minutes before bringing it into the boat, only to have it throw the hook and jump back into the deep water. Little-fat-pigeon rolled in laughter, holding his sides.

"What's so funny?" I asked, somewhat annoyed with our loss.

"Didn't you hear what he said?"

"No, I heard nothing."

"He said he was not going to feed Little-fat-pigeon today." That kind of humor takes some getting used to, but the Kuruaya do seem to respond to nature as though they are all part of the same family.

(The Indians respect nature as well, riding with it instead of fighting it the way non-Indians tend to do. They want to keep the forest like it is; they'll let others hunt and fish there, but if the guests build a house or plant,

2. Most Kuruayan families today have one home in town so the children can go to school, and one in the forest, which serves to supply some of their food.

122

they'll be killed. That has happened to several home-steaders across our river.)

One day on a fishing trip my Indian guide surprised me. We had paddled for four hours and had portaged eight times to reach the place where he wanted to fish in the morning, but now, as we prepared for a night on the open beach, I was reluctant to go to sleep in light of the fresh jaguar tracks all around us.

"What was this big jaguar doing here?" I asked.

"Hunting," was the too simple answer.

"Will he come back to hunt *us*?"

"No, he is friendly. This is not his time to be mean."

I wasn't sure the jaguar had gotten the message, but my son and I slept well and we were ready to fish by daylight. In two hours of heavy fishing we caught 150 pounds of large-mouth bass. With still much time left for good fishing, I reeled in my line and signaled my son to call it a day. Our guide couldn't understand.

"Why do you stop fishing? There is still much time left."

"We have all we can save," I answered. "More will only spoil on the way out."

"You are a very strange white man," my Indian friend replied.

On our way out of that wild country of rocks and rushing water, my friend turned into a quiet bay and beached the boat.

"The white man who does not waste fish will want to see this," he said as we climbed the sand. On top of the bank lay a large stone wheel. It was seven feet in diameter and more than three feet thick. Strange, beautiful carvings of stars and moon and other figures decorated its surface, whispering of a civilization of long ago. A flat part on the wheel looked like a base on which it once had stood. With the open palm of his hand my friend slapped the stone; it responded with the deep rumble of an ancient gong. If the wheel had been standing on its base, the sound would have carried for a great distance. In reverent tones the Indian asked questions I could not answer.

"Who were these people?" he said. "When did they live here? Where have they gone? They were gone long before my people came here."

Recorded history tells us very little about the Indians who lived along the Xingu River before the white man invaded their lands. History recorded by whites affirms that no great Indian civilizations existed in Brazil similar to those of the Incas of Peru. Most of the tribes seemed to have existed in small, widely-scattered groups that fought with each other and moved from place to place in search of food and protection from enemies.[3]

In 1614 the Portuguese arrived in Amazonia expecting to find riches. These pioneers were few and conditions difficult, so the Indians—necessary for a successful venture— were pressed into service. In time it became evident that Indians were not as adaptable to slave labor as slaves imported from Africa, so an additional element was added to the mixture making up modern Brazil.

In time Dutch and French adventurers penetrated the Amazon, establishing settlements and building forts. (The English also attempted to establish a foothold in the region.) Indians would camp near the forts for trading, and at times were forced into slave labor. Foreign men mixed freely with Indian women, and a new race came into existence. (A Dutch fort on the lower Xingu River was surrounded by the Portuguese in the mid-sixteen hundreds. The Dutch were ordered to surrender by dawn, or die. Next morning the fort was found to be empty of all defenders, and today one finds blond-haired, blue-eyed Indians on the Xingu.)

From stories I have been told, the Kuruaya once controlled the lands from the Iriri River to the big bend of the Xingu at Altamira. Constant warfare with their traditional

3. William Schurz, in *Brazil. The Infinite Country* (New York: Dutton, 1961), p. 75, states, "Brazil consisted of a myriad of small, isolated groups of Indians, mutually unacquainted or hostile. They found no bond of unity even in their linguistic affinities. . . . Each group tended to go its own way and to find its own primitive answers to the elementary problems of survival."

enemies, the Araras, weakened both tribes as fighting men were killed and women were carried away captive.[4] Both tribes were too weak to withstand the flood of hated Asuruni who drove them out of their lands, forcing the Araras to seek protection among the whites at Port Victoria and the Kuruaya among the settlers at Altamira. (The Asuruni, in turn, were driven out by the terrifying Kayapo who now rule from the upper Xingu to Altamira; the Araras in Port Victoria were rounded up, held in a stockade, and the men murdered—except for two who escaped. Today the Araras are known as wandering, hostile savages who kill on sight and avoid all contact with other people.)

One of my serious concerns regarding the Kuruaya is their lack of a father image. In all the tribes I have known on the Xingu, the father is master over the family, and he requires respect and obedience from the family members. But today, because of the wars, there are no old men who claim to be Kuruayan, and the young men—without a father image—take wives, father children, and work or hunt to provide the necessary food, but they seem to take no further responsibility for the family. They leave the training of the children to the women. The fathers of the Kuruaya who excelled as warriors in the forest have failed to find fulfillment in the new roles village living has placed upon them. Of all the men I have known of the Kuruaya, not one is a stable father, a steady worker, or a Christian.

Excessive individualism and desire to show personal strength is characteristic of Kuruayan men. Little-fat-pigeon and Raimundo came to work for me when I began construction on our home. Exhibiting powerful, shining bodies with beautiful muscles, these two stood out from

4. The severity of Indian wars can best be noted by the fact that I have never seen one Kuruaya man of my age. The oldest I have found are thirty years old or less. The fathers are gone! Another measure of the intensity of those wars is the fear and hate which come upon the old women as they relive the experiences while talking with me.

125

the rest of the construction crew. They worked together, but didn't like to help each other with the heavy loads, each choosing rather to make a show of his individual strength while the other watched. A tall palm tree had to come down to make room for my house. I put the two Kuruayans on the job, as they didn't like working with the other members of the crew.

"Why do you want to cut down this tree?" Little-fat-pigeon asked. "It gives food, and is good."

"I want to put my house where the tree stands," I answered.

"Why not put your house somewhere else?"

"There isn't enough room on the lot. The tree will have to go."

But I could see that my Indian workers could not understand how a house could be more important than a tree that gave food. I then tried to explain how I wanted the job done.

"Dig around the roots. Dig deep. Then cut the roots. When the tree falls, it will pull most of the roots out of the ground."

"You want the tree out and the roots also?" Raimundo asked.

"Yes."

"Does it matter how we do it?" he asked.

"No. Do it your way if you like." And the two strong Indians took turns all day—one displaying his strength while the other watched.

Over the years I grew close to Raimundo. I taught him to paint and to fix the jeep, and I gave him several jobs on construction projects. I helped him learn a profession and got him a good job in town. But Raimundo was never happy just working. Each evening he sat on the bank of the Xingu at sunset, looking sadly at the forests beyond. Twice he fathered children, but a family seemed to give him little satisfaction. Professional soccer gave him a chance to show his power and skill, but this too provided only brief fulfillment. Raimundo asked many questions about Christianity, but never seemed ready to commit

126

himself to following Christ. He became very sad, began drinking heavily, and went away. He has become another of the faceless fathers of the Kuruaya.[5]

The traditional role of the Kuruayan male is one of power, authority, and outstanding physical strength. The good man is one who provides well for his family by hunting, fishing, and planting the necessary crops. He protects his family from enemies and he teaches his sons how to become good members of the tribe.

But the modern Kuruayan man does not measure up to these ideal standards. His father is gone and the image has faded. He has been driven from his holy land and forced to live among strangers. The whites look down on him as inferior. The forests call, but they now belong to someone else. His wife and children need him, but his children have—or will soon have—a better education than he has. Why should they respect him when he doesn't hold his own with the whites around him? The easiest way is to become one of the faceless fathers and go away. Long trips into the forest, up the Xingu, along the Iriri, on to unknown lands and unknown tribes—and the fathers escape the role they cannot or will not fill.

The traditional role of the Kuruayan woman is one of obedience, hard work, and dedicated care of husband and children. She harvests the crops her man has planted, prepares the food he brings home, and gathers dry wood for the fire. She also makes whatever clothing is needed. Ideally, she is a good follower.

But the traditional role no longer fits. Kuruayan women—little girls as young as twelve and thirteen—live with almost any man who wants them. They have children, and are left by the men who wanted pleasure without responsibility. Then they return to the family until another man comes along who wants them. Often three children

5. Although Little-fat-pigeon was able to give up his love for heavy drinking, and, in time, became a Christian, tuberculosis took him before he reached the age of thirty and another father of the Kuruaya became a faceless memory.

will have three fathers, none of whom are Kuruayan. (The children are all Kuruayan, however, because the mother feels her identity with the tribe.) The old mother, in the absence of a father image, takes over the leadership—and leads her family well. In addition to holding the family together, she trains, clothes, and educates the children and grandchildren, and teaches them the values of the tribe.

As I remember the strong women of the Kuruaya, the face of *Dona* (Madam) Francisca comes immediately to mind. Merry and I stopped for lunch one day near an Indian house. Large mango trees from a nearby grove offered welcome shade from the noontime sun, and the owner of the house and grove, a woman in her late fifties, brought us ripe mangos and fresh water.

From Francisca's large house of poles with grass roof there streamed a group of beautiful youngsters. Francisca's larger family consists of twenty children and grandchildren still at home, and several unmarried daughters who work in Altamira and who regularly bring fatherless children back to their mother for care and training. A state primary school has been constructed near her home, and her grow-ing family fills the classes.

Impressed with Francisca's unusual hospitality, Merry and I offered to return with Bible filmstrips and music if she would allow us to come. She also invited Roman Catholics, Baptists, and Pentecostals to visit and teach in her village, and although she was pleased when her hus-band and several of the children became followers of Christ,[6] as a respected shaman for many years, Francisca remained firm in her Indian religion.

After about two years of monthly visits, Francisca began

6. During the six years we visited Francisca's family, fifteen children became Christians, as did some of the non-Indian neighbors. One son, Geraldo, and a grandson, Jean, became Christians during the early days of our work in the village. They are two of the brightest, most intelligent boys I have ever taught. After completing primary school in the village, I helped finance their studies in the Altamira school system, buying books, uniforms, and necessary equip-ment. In return, they worked in my yard every Saturday. Both are much better students than workers, but I offered to help them attend university if they would continue to show promise and avoid the vices that so often destroy an Indian's progress toward productive assimilation.

asking many questions about the Christian God. When I told her about my own experience of being confronted by Christ and called to follow him, and of being guided by God's Spirit since that turning point in my life, I believe she understood.

"I don't like the padre or those other pastors who come here," Francisca said one day. "They all want me to join their church and follow their ways. I like the ways of my people better. Don't you want me to join your church?"

Both the Catholic priest and the Baptist pastor who visited the village were friends of mine, so I was careful with my reply. "Francisca, if you want to join my church, I would be happy to have you as a sister in the family, but my church does not save anyone. The important thing is to be a member of the tribe of those who follow Jesus. That makes all the difference now, and in the life beyond."

"The others say I must stop talking with my people. What do you say, *Seu Paulo*?" she asked.

"I have never talked with the spirits of your people. I don't know them, and they don't know me. What do you say? Do you talk with good spirits or bad?"

"Some are good and some are not good," she replied.

"Have you talked with 'The Big Indian?' " I asked.

Real fear came into her face, and she answered, "I have seen him! He is bad! I will not serve him!"

("The Big Indian" is an evil spirit known and feared among the Indians and spiritists in Brazil. Some say he is the devil himself. He offers supernatural power to any who will serve him completely, without reserve. And he collects a high price of his slaves in return for mystic knowledge and strange powers. It is commonly said among the spiritists that the only escape for those who have surrendered to his power is in the name of Christ.)

"Francisca, I cannot tell you with whom you can speak. The Bible says that those who are filled with God's Spirit do not need to talk with spirits of the dead, and should not do so. I can only say to you that I met Christ, and follow him, and God has put his Spirit in me to tell me what I should do and to whom I should look for direction and protection. He will do the same for you, if you really want him."

On my next visit a couple months later I encountered a very different Francisca. There was a deep peace and a new joy shining in her dark face.

"I am a Christian," she said. "I follow Christ. I am guided by the Great Spirit. I worship only God."

It would not be honest to say that all Francisca's problems have been solved. She still has as many as before, but now she has supernatural help—and with it, hope! Although the mighty Xingu still withholds its secrets from those who live beside it, for Francisca, the "Faceless Father" of the Kuruaya now has a face.

And we, who with unveiled faces all reflect the Lord's glory, are being transformed into his likeness with ever-increasing glory, which comes from the Lord, who is the Spirit (2 Cor. 3:17-18).